"The Brand Bucket® provided us with
mission. Many of the conclusions reflec
thinking, and the approach brought this into a workable
foundation and swiftly translated into our online and offline
communications."

Julie Molloy, Marcoms Director, Bookham Technology plc ✓

"The Brand Bucket® has been working for us for almost six years
now on a full range of projects building our brand, corporate
identity, web and marketing activity. The approach is
innovative, directional and measurable and now you can see the
daffodil almost everywhere in the community."

Chris Dainty, Director of PR and Marketing,
Marie Curie Cancer Care

"The Brand Bucket® approach has worked with us to redefine
our brand, developing a new marketing effort producing a
positive response from our target market. For us, working with
this approach is a long term strategy for growth and success."

Allan Lee, Director, Abracadabra services Ltd

"I thought I'd seen everything and The Brand Bucket® was just
another approach but after reading this book this is one of the
most complete methodologies for marketing I've come across.
Barnaby is a purple cow."

Chris Hughes, Vistage Chair

"This book confirms Barnaby as a truly Mad Man of the 21st
Century."

Stuart Bull

"As Chief Financial Officer in a law firm, this is the first time I have fully understood how marketing relates to the numbers in my firm. Now working for us today."

Geeves Silva FCCA, Hodders Law

"The Brand Bucket® approach enables any organisation to harness its value proposition and create strong brand marketing. Highly recommended."

Chris Lyons, Network Housing Group Chair

the
brand
bucket®

make your marketing work

Barnaby Wynter

To my wife Meriel,
thank you

First published in 2010 by Management Books 2000 Ltd
Forge House, Limes Road
Kemble, Cirencester
Gloucestershire, GL7 6AD, UK
Tel: 0044 (0) 1285 771441
Fax: 0044 (0) 1285 771055
Email: info@mb2000.com
Web: www.mb2000.com

British Library Cataloguing in Publication Data is available

ISBN 9781852526528

CONTENTS

1

MAKE YOUR MARKETING WORK

"Only 20% of my marketing is working only I don't know which 20% it is."

If you are using traditional marketing methods you could be wasting up to 80% of your marketing spend. In the last five years the way marketing works has fundamentally changed.

We have all become conditioned to use the world around us in a different way to make buying decisions.

No longer does TV represent the only way we get our new information, or the centre break in Coronation Street deliver 22 million attentive viewers. No longer do people stare expectantly out of their windows waiting for the army of newspaper boys to throw the daily paper onto their front door steps. No more that sense of colour emerging on the horizon as roadside *There are now over 440 TV stations in the UK alone* billboard brightens a bleak concrete landscape. Today we are bombarded by literally thousands of different media.

Improvements in print technology mean anything that can carry a message probably has one on it.

If you are not tripping over it, you are drinking from it, leaning on it or squashed against it.

At home, on the way to work, at work, on the way home again, when you are out, when you are in. It's message madness. On average we receive over 4,000 new marketing messages every day. To cope with this brand noise, we've all learnt to be very selective, to only absorb what we want to absorb. Actually we've learnt to ignore it.

And this has led to a fundamental change in the way marketing works so that now people take in messages differently. *No longer is marketing interruptive, it is now interactive.* Brand messages no longer cut through some other form of activity but are invited in.

The consumer is in control. A brand can only get to communicate with them when and how they want it to do so.

Broadcast media advertising no longer works. Consumers are winding past the commercials via the remote or simply channel-hopping to find something else they like. They are absorbing "sound bite" editorial in a free news-sheets or preselecting a highly targeted trade or a hobbyist magazine or accepting "opt-in" email shots or even engaging others via social networking platforms. Many are now inputting keywords into search engines or selecting an app from their mobile phone to find what they are looking for. **Today's information is by request,** so brands are by request too.

In 1985, SAAB Automotive commissioned a large piece of research to establish how people bought motor cars. The resulting work led to the creation of **The Brand Bucket**®, a six-step decision-making model that turns prospects into valued long-term consumers.

Actively used every day since then, The Brand Bucket® has been applied to businesses and organisations worldwide, working every day to enable those businesses achieve their sales goals for over 2,500 different products and services.

Today the methodology is more effective than ever as it cuts a swathe through much of the nonsense that is peddled in the marketing industry.

The approach makes sure all of the money you spend talking to your target market is focused on informing people why they should buy from you and this continues even after they have bought from you. √

If you want to find out how to make your marketing work, read on. If you want to stay with the old ways then don't. This will not make pleasant reading. Do please pass it on to someone who might like it, though.

So how has marketing changed?

In the early days of the consumer age, inventors and entrepreneurs could create a new product or service, stick it on television or in the newspaper and know that literally millions of people would see their new offer and if they were interested go down to the local high street and buy it.

As a result a thriving advertising-led marketing industry emerged, built around the concept of demographics, the segmentation of target markets by customer characteristics – broadly age, sex, social class and income. When there were limited outlets for advertising, all you needed was as large a loudhailer as you could afford and as long as your offer stacked up you were in the money.

There has been more technological development in the last 15 years than in the whole history of mankind before.

Over time, simply shouting at people became less appealing so we saw the emergence of "creativity", the creation of ideas that engaged us in different ways. Ideas that were designed to make us laugh, to make us think, to make us feel sexy, to make us feel inadequate. All aimed to cut through against the competitors.

But as creativity took hold, brand-owners found that simply

shouting only worked if you had a big, big budget, so to enable those with smaller budgets to have a go, the media started to segment further and as they gained more knowledge about viewers and readers we saw more and more TV channels, newspapers and magazines. Still all demographically led.

This was aided by technology.

Firstly print technology improved so new alternative media started to appear on a more regular basis. Very quickly people were printing on almost anything and everything.

Consumers initially reacted well to all these new products with their **Unique Selling Point (USP)** messages appearing in Unique Selling Places, so of course it led to more and more of everything.

Secondly, new technology meant that new products and services were created at a rate never seen before and now there were a plethora of choices where once there may have only been a few. From washing detergents and bread to holidays and cars, a vast array of alternatives. We all entered into a new era in marketing, an age when because of choice an ad didn't automatically lead to a sale.

This was when we started to see a shift away from the **clumsy demographic planning tool** to a much more sophisticated approach to targeting.

Now brand-owners were beginning to think about how the medium could help the message. The media loved it and massaged their rates to meet this new level of "sophistication": people who like sports read the sports pages, let's charge more; people who are in business will read the business pages, let's charge more; people who like fishing will read this angling magazine, let's charge more.

Media-owners got greedier. Brand-owners saw less return from their marketing. Consumers started to filter out all these messages everywhere but were trapped because there were few other sources of news about all these new products and services.

Very quickly the USP was dead

Then the internet joined the party. A dream for the information-hungry geeks until the search engine arrived. Now consumers could purposefully ignore all these messages coming at them from all directions knowing that there was a tool that they could control to get the information they required, how they want it and when they want it.

Demographics …. dead!

The consumers are in control. And because they are in control they no longer accept simply being told what is good, they want to *decide* what is good because there is always an alternative that merits consideration.

Today consumers source their information in a totally different way to the way brand-owners want to tell it.

A brand-owner wants to convey the rational side of their offer and get as much money for it as possible. The consumer wants to understand the value they'll get when they spend their hard-earned cash.

> *It is not from the benevolence of the butcher, the brewer, or the baker that we expect our dinner, but from their regard to their own interest. We address ourselves, not to their humanity, but to their self-love, and never talk to them of our own necessities, but of their advantages.*
>
> Adam Smith, *The Wealth of Nations* (1776)

Only marketing can bring these two opposing attitudes together. Not by shouting, not by disruptive or interruptive communication but by listening, sharing and interacting with the consumer throughout the decision-making journey.

From initial contact all the way through to loyalty, **your marketing needs to engage with the psychographic profile** of the consumer not the demographic.

This engagement means listening to, talking with and managing the way your targets feel as they move towards purchase and especially after they have purchased.

The Brand Bucket® guides this process from beginning to end ensuring that at every level of the marketing mix your brand is working towards making you money.

The history of The Brand Bucket®

In 1984, SAAB invited their agency Humphrey Barker Bull to undertake a research project to identify the steps people went through when buying a new motor car. After six months of consumer research, Stuart Bull derived a six step approach which captured the very essence of the sales decision-making process.

It brought together the emotional decisions, the rational decisions and the metrics that underpin these and turn prospects into long-term loyal customers.

In providing this framework for a communication plan for SAAB, the agency were able to quickly and effectively create the award-winning launch campaign for the SAAB in the UK featuring a Viggen fighter plane racing a SAAB 900.

By applying The Brand Bucket® to the whole communication mix this story was applied to SAAB at every level of their marketing.

Stuart was a career-long planner by trade and soon realised that the application of The Brand Bucket® was universal, with the potential to work across all the products and services that were with the agency at the time including the likes of FEDEX, Uniroyal Tyres, the AA, Carlsberg, Halfords and Eurostar.

HBB become KHBB, and in 1995 the agency was sold to the

Saatchi brothers becoming "K" in the process.

Stuart kept the Brand Bucket® concept, and realising that the advertising world was changing and that its role in the marketing mix was showing signs of decline, he immediately set up an agency to specifically service the whole marketing mix as guided by The Brand Bucket®.

The launches of Deutsche Post, First Telecom and rebrands for The Children's Society saw the application of The Brand Bucket® come to life, and with continued work for The AA, Eurostar and Carlsberg the agency began to grow.

As the online arena took its place at the marketing table, the agency evolved to integrate both the online and offline arenas with the first expression of this being the launch of E*Trade in 1997/8 which became one of the largest online brokers in the world.

Stuart retired in 2001. That year the Brand Bucket® methodology was trademarked and with over 2,500 products and services to its name, The Brand Bucket® continues to be used every day to drive the sales for brands all over the world.

2

BEFORE WE START – WHAT IS BRAND?

This might seem an odd question given the title of this book but one of the key outputs of successful marketing is that you are left with a brand.

Make no mistake this should never ever be at the expense of sales but if you have created a brand then the chances are you will have achieved one of the most valuable indicators that your business plan works. And yet when people are asked what brand is, whether in the "brand" industry or as simple consumers, no-one appears to be able to describe what a brand is.

Brand is not:

- An ID
- The logo
- A perception
- A belief
- Quality

In fact after asking over 2,000 marketing people over a period of ten years there now exists a list of 73 different, and yet quite tenable, answers. Try and answer the question yourself. If we cannot define what a brand is, then how can we use marketing effectively to help us create a brand? Other efforts to generate sales are well just sales.

So if it is "brand" that distinguishes marketing from sales, what is it?

The question was put to a number of people who had been working with The Brand Bucket® for over 15 years. A collection of staff with 148 years of direct experience in creating brands failed entirely to come up with a definition (and indeed failed to add to the list!). A 3½-week desktop research programme of over 200 marketing books, 80 of which, like this one, had "Brand" in the book title, also drew a blank.

This was scary.

How could an industry that so liberally uses the word "Brand" not be able to throw up a decent definition? More importantly, how did anyone know what they were doing when it came to creating a brand?

The answer is of course that everyone "gets away with it", and this is quite clearly another reason why up to 80% of marketing doesn't work and salespeople struggle to understand marketing people.

Let's change that now.

The trouble with most definitions is that they seek to describe the features of the subject rather than the outcomes. We need to be certain that our definitions are focused on outcome. So let's start with a working concept for marketing:

MARKETING = SALES + BRAND

Logic dictates that we can also define sales as follows:

SALES = MARKETING – BRAND

Surely we can now define brand:

BRAND = MARKETING – SALES

But this quite clearly doesn't go far enough for "Brand". There is something more to "Brand" than this.

Brand is owned by a product or service, it is both tangible and intangible; it is a combination of both the rational and emotional; it is a degree of desirability, it represents equity in a business. It is in the mind of the customer. It is a perception. So what is it really? No wonder the world of brand is full of bull.

It is simply not good enough to continue to use marketing in your business without understanding that the output is primarily sales and brand.

So here's a definition of brand that was created by a group of Brand Bucket® practitioners and has been in use since 2002, the year of discovering that brand had no definition:

Brand is every experience that affects the relationship between a product or service and its consumer.

Let's look at this statement in detail.

1. Relationship between a product or service and its consumer

This is by no means an ordinary relationship. Firstly, it is between what your company sells and its consumer.

A consumer is a person who uses your product or at least owns a right to use your product. To do so they should have parted with some money. Now this is the crux of this relationship. It is one which has value whether monetary or not. For the consumer it is a relationship that they value more than the money in their pocket. For a business-owner it is a relationship that delivers that value without it costing, at worst, the same as it takes to deliver the product, or at best a lot *less* than it takes to make and sell the product leaving a bit behind, often called profit.

Now this is not meant to sound patronising but how often do you read marketing books that talk about profit – gross, net or otherwise? Rarely, never?

So this relationship is key to the profit from your marketing.

2. Every experience that affects the relationship

Now to build this relationship you need to engage with your prospect and make sure that every time your prospect comes in contact with your product or service, it is in a way that strengthens the bond between your business and their value perception of what you are offering.

In other words every time they experience your brand story, make sure that the experience **"affects"** how the prospect feels about you and helps them understand why they should buy from you.

Leave no stone unturned. From the way you answer the phone to how you offer a hot drink, to your product presentation and advertising, your packaging, your user guides, your contracts, your everything.

Any point of contact represents an opportunity to get your message across in a way that affects the relationship. So every time a prospect comes in contact with a product or service, each and every interaction should guide that prospect towards a deeper understanding of your value proposition – what makes you worth buying.

If you have a boiler, how long have you had it, and can you name the brand? Can you name the brand of car you drive?

This must not stop at prospects either; it must be applied to customers too. This is generally easier if you are selling a car but much harder if you are selling insurance products or a boiler where daily interaction is less likely.

Everything you produce should be produced in a way that has the power to influence the purchaser's decision-making process,

every experience.

Just think about the prospect journey and what it is like to be a consumer.

Think about it at every level and design that experience in a way that influences what people believe about you. Have you taught all your suppliers about your value proposition as well as your staff? Make no mistake, if you haven't your brand is weakened, and if you are not in control of how your business is portrayed then someone else will be. If they are your competition then... well, you know the answer to this don't you.

It is said that the average time from specification to full production in China is as little as 3 weeks!

In a world where everything can be copied instantaneously, it is imperative that you create a relationship with your customers that is unique to you and works for them not just for you.

By adding this relationship to your sales process you will have a brand.

Marketing is the toolkit to build the relationship.

Time to unpack the toolkit and lay everything out on the floor.

3

THE 4 STEPS TO MAKE MARKETING WORK AND CREATE YOUR BRAND

Bringing any brand to market, no matter whether it is totally new or a revamp of an existing product or service, provides the brand-owner with exactly the same challenges and yet it seems that many marketers feel it's necessary to reinvent the rules.

The four steps are simple really:

Step 1. Get your value proposition right

People will only pay you when they believe that the product or service you offer is worth more than the money in their pocket. So you have to **define your value proposition** before you embark on any marketing.

Over 80% of businesses have not defined their value proposition leading to untold waste in expenditure on marketing. Unless you understand what you are selling to people, those same people cannot (and will not) buy from you. A clever idea from your marketing agency will not cover up the fact that you have not defined what you are selling.

So where does this value proposition come from? The answer is rarely, if ever, from research. Asking what customers want of you is like asking a child if they want more sweets. The answer will make a whole lot of sense but will not be the answer you need.

Asking a non-user of your product or service is like asking a child if they want sweets in the first place. It sounds good so why shouldn't I, they wouldn't be asking if it wasn't ok.

The truth is that the value proposition comes from one place only. The business itself.

Luciano Benetton famously said: "Communication should never be conceived from outside the organisation but conceived from the heart of the organisation."

That heart is with you, the reader of this book. Only you know what makes the sale. It is often why most business-owners are the best salesmen.

The trouble is that over time this "sales story" is diluted by the day-to-day rigour of running a business and as organisations grow with more people "doing the business", this message can be lost altogether.

This sales story has to be retrieved for successful marketing because it is from this story that messages at each level of the decision-making process can be told, guiding prospects towards the point where they value the story enough to buy what the organisation is selling.

> **KEY ACTION: Define your value proposition. This is the foundation of your marketing. How to do this is in Chapter 12.**

Step 2. Audit how you are telling your story

Once you have defined your value proposition and created your story you now need to audit how you are portraying that story throughout your business.

But there is something you have to do first. Before you start this you need to decide to whom you are going to tell your story, because if you don't, then much of your marketing will end up being wasted.

You cannot be all things to everyone so the more focused this targeting can be the more effective the marketing.

Historically this has resulted in a demographic description of your target audience. For example, this might be high net worth individuals, living in South East, aged between 35 and 54 years, married with children with a 60:40 bias male to female, with a household income of 100K plus and a disposable income of 25K per annum.

Not uncommon, that description is about as useful as a ladle in a rowing boat. If you use it enough, you'll get some movement and you might even be able to drink some water but to be honest there are better ways.

The reason these target market definitions prevail is because they match up how the owners of broadcast media audit their media and it is easy to find the data to support the above profile.

Think about how many forms and applications you have completed to join up to things, where you have to answer the gender, age and income questions. This is the information media-owners use to persuade advertisers to use their medium.

In the information age that we live in, this most basic of tools is both woefully inadequate and indeed almost crass for today's business marketer because it enables broadcast strategies to prevail when we now know that this process is neither invasive nor persuasive.

On top of this, society has become more integrated culturally; we have become part of a global economy and thankfully the gaps between the men and women, colour and creed have closed (although still not close enough yet to ensure equality). As more and more products and services focus on appealing to specific target markets the use of these demographic tools cannot work.

So we have to work harder with another recognised profile tool when talking about our target market – **the psychographic profile**.

The psychographic profile is not a description of who the target market is but how they feel; what's worrying them and what they are hoping to do about it; where they are looking for the answers and why, how they can improve their quality of life.

These are **the values of the target prospect**. Now you have a willing audience for your own value proposition, your marketing can be focused on getting your message into the places where and when these people are more receptive to your value proposition. Understanding how to talk to your prospect and not just how to reach them will also have a major impact on your creative work too!

Does it really make sense to try and sell cornflakes at 6pm or beer in a morning paper or IT consultancy at an arts festival or music retailing in a library or shoes on a bus-side or a car on a 48-sheet poster? All these strategies can be sold using demographics but when you start to think psychographically, you begin to see how there might be better ways to spend hard-earned profits and reduce the wastage.

The best way to profile your target market is to describe them as you would to a friend who you were recommending for a meet-up. Not:

John is 5 foot 9 inches with dark hair and likes to wear multicoloured t-shirts, plays golf and has a wife and two children. You should talk to him.

A better description tends to be more humanistic than that:

He's a great bloke, really easy to get on with and has a great sense of humour. He will know how to help you. I'll get him to call you.

Make no mistake if you describe your brand in the same way, everyone who comes into contact with that brand, whether staff, suppliers or prospects and consumers, will become engaged so much more effectively.

By describing your target market in psychographic terms, suddenly judging the tonality of your message, the way it is conveyed and how to choose media can help your message be understood more easily and more quickly.

Does this mean we need hundreds of psychographic profiles because we have all sorts of different consumers? Fortunately not.

A psychographic profile is confined by the value proposition of your product or service. The way we feel about **fast** food is not the same as we feel about **fast** cars and **fast**-drying paint. With your value proposition in place we can now concentrate on attracting prospects and meeting their needs with value statements that *they* will want to buy specifically from you. Now we need a cunning plan.

> **KEY ACTION: Work out your target audience by identifying what they are thinking and feeling, not who or what they are.**

Case study: Deutsche Post

When we were asked to help launch Deutsche Post in UK, the first thing was to get a good understanding of the psychographic of the target market – the mailrooms of major corporations who used Royal Mail.

Everyone loved Royal Mail, they had grown up with it and had positive associations with the brand. After all, it had delivered their birthday cards and presents. Good old Postman Pat, our friend. But when it came to business there were some doubts about the effectiveness of the service, especially when delivering abroad.

In presenting Deutsche Post as an alternative, it would be clear from the name that this was a German Postal service, so no need to do too much to raise awareness. The service was likely to be efficient and precise but lacked empathy and that sense of British humour that is present in mailrooms in the UK.

From this psychographic profile Deutsche Post was launched by sending out 20,000 branded towels supported by the line **"Trust the Germans to Get You There First"** a play on the sun-lounger experience of many while on holiday. By using the psychographic profile of the audience, mailrooms were buzzing as they jumped around with the towel they'd received from the Germans at Deutsche Post.

Step 3. Put together a measurable plan

"I know what works so we'll do more of that." A common view of the person holding the purse strings. "I don't need a plan."

How many journeys do you go on without deciding on a

destination and, if you don't know how to get there, a map of some sort? Marketing (and for that matter business) is no different. You need a plan.

The trouble with a make-it-up-as-you-go-along self-made plan is that you can only go the route you already know. Great if that's the only route but not so good when there are many different ways to go. Marketing is especially prone to offering literally hundreds of paths to follow to achieve a plan.

So the answer: Call in the experts.

And so a marketing plan emerges with all the old friends Public Relations (PR), advertising, exhibitions or promotions. This plan has only one type of interested party, the media-owners, none of whom take any responsibility for getting you sales. Prospects certainly, enquiries maybe, conversions? No, that's down to you!

When was the last time you sat down and just watched "what's on" television? OK, when was the last time you watched television at all? Describe the commercials you saw. Name three brands you remember seeing. Now please sign off this media plan.

This isn't being clever, it's simply that no-one in the broadcast world wants you to find out (yet) that much of what is being recommended cannot avoid huge waste or deliver guaranteed results (until they've found a new way to protect their revenues).

It is now clear that prospects control the messages they are happy to receive. We've all learnt to do this because everything that can carry a marketing message has got one. Add that to all the other information we are bombarded with as individuals, and to stay sane we have to screen out all uninvited marketing messages until we are ready to start a new decision-making process.

Using your psychographic profile you can start your plan by qualifying, maintaining and adding together all of the ways you are communicating your brand and are getting it right already.

Very few businesses use this as a starting point for beginning the conversation for sales. This audit should cover all of the things that prospects and consumers come into contact with at any time that affect the ongoing perception that you are providing value.

Once you have grasped The Brand Bucket® you will see where there are gaps in the decision-making process and this leads to the second element of the plan. Plugging those gaps to ensure the journey for your prospect to becoming a loyal consumer is seamless.

Finally and most importantly, your plan should have a sales target not a budget. This is the real challenge. A plan to deliver sales not spend the budget. A plan that relates investment to return in sales. A plan that comes alive through numbers: numbers of prospects; numbers of enquiries; numbers proposals or trials and test drives; numbers of conversions; numbers of purchases, numbers of repeat purchases; numbers of referrals. No plan should be without a sense of these.

> **KEY ACTION: Get a plan to communicate your value proposition. What works already, what doesn't and what's missing.**

Case study: Marie Curie Cancer Care

A good plan should first include all the things you are getting right already. In 2002 Marie Curie Cancer Care undertook a rebrand. More people associated the daffodil with cancer than the charity to a point where the brief for the rebrand even asked the question should the daffodil be retained. A brand audit revealed that the charity was using 49 different daffodils across all their materials. Today they use just one.

It appears on everything they do and can be seen on many lapels during daffodil month each year raising valuable funds to help the charity undertake their important work.

Step 4. Execute and measure your plan

Having identified what works already for you, now you need to add in the marketing tools that will fill your bucket with sales.

Some of you reading the book may have come across the "sales funnel" as a piece of marketing speak. This is an expression derived from a broadcast industry where marketing would pour people into your sales funnel and create leads. Once in the sales funnel these leads become the responsibility of the sales department and no longer anything to do with the marketing department. Their job done.

These leads need to be converted into customers by getting them to part with their cash – the sales bit, the mucky bit, and often the area of friction between the marketing department and the sales force. Because no-one took responsibility for the handover of the leads, they would shoot out through the hole in the bottom of the funnel and often never be seen again as the marketing process stopped and the sales process did not begin.

The broadcast marketer has created cut-through, disruptive, single-minded, often humorous or image-led attractors in the form of TV commercials or double-page-spread press ads. The salesman has to unhook the prospect from this obviously unrelated relationship, find out what the prospect wants, portray the product or service in a way that the prospect will value more than the money in their pocket and convert them into a consumer. So much easier if marketing wasn't in the way!

The use of funnel thinking is another factor responsible for the 80% waste of marketing spend. **Marketing should never stop**. Certainly not for prospects and not for consumers either and sales should work in parallel with marketing at all times. More of this later. You need an approach that keeps as many of your prospects and customers in your business. **You need a bucket!**

To fill your bucket you must stop it springing leaks (metrically there are always some) and stop it overflowing, so you need to execute only *measurable* marketing, keeping track of its successes and failures, and readjust the plan to fit with the expectations of the business.

Now marketing spends can be monitored and minimised by adjusting the plan and the messaging.

KEY ACTION: Measure Everything.

4

INTRODUCING THE BRAND BUCKET®

How The Brand Bucket® Works

As mentioned earlier, The Brand Bucket® was developed to help SAAB understand how to convert people who had not heard of SAAB into loyal customers. Being a relatively new entrant into the UK market in 1985, this approach was to underpin their marketing actively for years to come. Indeed if you look at their marketing today, there are still signs of the learnings of The Brand Bucket® in play.

The Brand Bucket® is a definitive tool to **turn prospects into people who regularly use your product or service.** Traditional marketers like to call these customers, but this is a trap set by those who are seeking to appeal to the business-owner.

Customers are, by definition, people who have given your business "custom" – i.e. they have already bought from you. Knowing this, many businesses change their behaviour towards customers. After touting your purchase they then promptly ignore you once you have bought. Think banks, utilities, phone operators. Do you feel valued as a customer?

The Brand Bucket® maps out the **continuous decision-making process** as we change our purchase propensity from being a prospect right through to becoming a long-term loyal consumer. A fully paid-up consumer of your product or service will buy from you again and again if you look after them and even act as an advocate and recommend you to others.

These are **consumers with potential** or as you should think of them, potential consumers.

Your marketing plan should contain ongoing activity to keep up conversations with everyone who has any association with buying into or buying from you. For fully paid-up consumers as much as prospects.

> **KEY ACTION: Your marketing should be constantly active, talking to consumers with potential to either buy more or recommend you to others.**

Now a prospect is quite different to a consumer (potential customer).

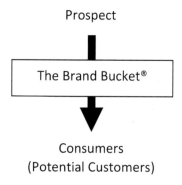

Sales and marketing plans are inspired by what is *known* about a business. They are often derived from an internal "company out" perception of what makes their product or service great, or research amongst existing users, lapsed users or non-users.

All very good but **prospects don't care.**

They don't care if you exist, what you offer or how you do it. They've got lives of their own. All being well, their lives are a constant balancing act between getting money, through work or otherwise, and spending money on things they need to live and things that make up quality of life. They don't want you to disrupt this balance. In fact they would prefer that you simply leave them alone. (It's partly why we all yearn for the countryside or the seaside. Back to nature means get away from man-made messaging that dominates all our lives. Stare out to sea. How many ads can you see? A mind at peace at last.)

Today, because of the impact of technology, transport and media, almost any physical item can carry a disruptive message. Live newsfeeds, printed words and images on everything, digital this and that. Buy me messages everywhere.

Because of this, prospects block out your marketing until they are ready to consider you, and only then do they give you the signals that they are ready to enter into a conversation with you. **The Brand Bucket® identifies precisely when a prospect is ready to talk with you**, how they want to talk to you and what you should do next to communicate your value proposition to the point where they will part with their hard-earned cash. So let's examine the six proven stages of engagement in detail.

The 6 Steps

First used in 1985, The Brand Bucket® has been continuously used to map out the decision-making process for purchasing products and services across the globe. The approach works as a filtration process to overcome information overload, defining the journey prospects go through as they make a decision to buy. As it is applied, The Brand Bucket® ensures that prospect decisions are directed towards the product or service you want to sell.

STEP 1 – Create Awareness

The first job of any marketing communication plan is to tell those who you wish to be consumers that you are there – to build the awareness of the product or service.

Obvious certainly but, in isolation, this is not enough to change people's behaviour. It is a fundamental first step to the process of buying because it sets up the relationship and begins the journey of increasing people's disposition towards you for the simple reason that you now exist in their world.

However if that is all you do, people, when challenged, will simply say they have heard of you.

Just because you exist doesn't mean much to people without giving them additional information to judge whether you are offering a valued relationship that will get those same people to engage with you further.

More importantly if a customer can only recall your name, your logo or your advertising line and nothing else about you, they will assume that they have rejected your advances previously. In their minds eye you will fall into the category of "not for me". This is a very dangerous place to be as it means you now have to overcome a communication legacy which you yourself have created.

Perversely, the more powerful your iconography or name, the more likely you are to have been attracted by the awareness building industry via public relations (PR), sponsorship or advertising. As a result your marketing plan will have created more reject thinking amongst your prospects.

For example think of names like The Sock Shop, Tie Rack, The Pound Shop, Yo Sushi, Beefeater among many, many others. These are the type of names that require additional experience or marketing to explain how their offer is more than that which the name conveys.

Raising awareness on its own is one of the most wasteful ways of using marketing funds. It is imperative that the journey for the prospect continues on to step two.

> **KEY ACTION: Tell the people who you would like to buy your product that you are there.**

STEP 2 – Image Match

Having created the awareness we must now consider what we want our customers to "feel" about us. In this way they can align the brand to their own lifestyle.

Create a sustainable image and the prospect stays in the relationship with you.

The strongest image anyone has of anything is the one of themselves. Not surprising since you have been with yourself every moment since you were conceived. Your own image is extensively nurtured and cared for. From the moment we are awake until the moment we go back to sleep (indeed some argue even whilst we are asleep) we constantly feed the image of our own self by establishing values and knowledge through experience.

Indeed, as our image develops, we go through the Maslow's

Hierarchy of Needs, a series of behavioural states that result from our life state. As we negotiate through each day, our need state changes. One minute we are crossing the road and physical health is key (a good time to buy a holiday on the side of a taxi?), the next we are sharing a coffee break with our best friend who is going through an emotional time (a good time to buy car insurance?), the next minute we are reading a company report (a good time to buy a case of wine?) and finally we are attending the PTA meeting (a good time to buy a car?).

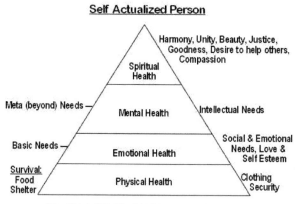

Maslow's idea was that you couldn't commit yourself totally to the higher levels until you had satisfied your needs on the lower levels.

Abraham Maslow's Hierarchy of needs

Our need state changes literally minute to minute.
Blasting us with messages that have no relevance is not the best use of marketing funds. To make your marketing effective you need to communicate your image in a way that is relevant to the appropriate need state and it must be designed to generate the response: *"I see where you fit into my life."*

If your marketing does not elicit this response, people will reject the relationship as not for them or become attracted to other stronger promises of relationship that service the constant need to support their own personal image.

Mirror Mirror on the wall who makes me fairest of them all?

In the Western World, how many homes or hotels can you think of where you cannot find a mirror? It is a fundamental need for almost everybody to constantly check their image physically as well as emotionally too.

> **KEY ACTION:** 'Emotional' values must be identified and reflected in your brand communication campaign. They are the heart of your brand.

Brand image only works when it carries an emotional promise that meets the needs of the person to whom you are selling. It works best when you leave people with a positive disposition to the value of your brand in a way that makes them feel better about themselves.

The stronger this emotional attachment to your brand the less likely a prospect is to be attracted to another brand.

That said, if you only rely on emotional response then you'll find that when their "real world" kicks back in, that same prospect will "forget" your brand unless continually reminded of the feeling.

Because of this, many business-owners find themselves being convinced by hungry media-owners that they need to continually "advertise" their message. This supposedly ensures that they are continuously present in front of their prospect so that when their real world applies to the product, there they are. Logical, of course. But what they don't tell you is about the waste.

Waste that results from the fact that they have no idea what the need state is of the people consuming their media, reducing their chances of catching a prospect in buying mode. Add to this the fact that a significant proportion of viewers, readers and/or listeners don't even fall into your prospect category and you can see why broadcast media has become increasingly ineffective. It is here where the feeding frenzy of media-owners appears. Broadcast, broadcast, broadcast. The net result is a disproportionate advertising spend, often with no tangible results when it comes to sales.

Even though a prospect may have an emotional disposition towards your product, they will not simply buy there and then. There's still a lot of real world to take place before they are able to execute a purchase!

Emotional reasons alone are not enough to make a purchase decision. We all need more information.

In nature, as we all know, the decision when confronted with danger is "fight or flight".

This most basic of decisions is governed by a split second analysis of your "chances". Can you fight and win, and if not can you outrun your opposition? Are your weapons more substantial than your opponent's or can you get to a place of safety first?

All this needs additional rational information. The human brain is amazing and in those situations we are able to assimilate the data around us to decide if we stand and fight or get the hell out of there. I'll worry about the impact on the quality of my life after survival.

Buying things follows exactly the same pattern and because we have time to evaluate the impact of a buying decision on our self image, we all use rational information to inform this decision. Only then do we decide whether we need you or not.

Brand-owners often spend most of their money simply telling you they are there in a way that makes you feel good about them and then leave you without any real understanding of what they do. Try and think of TV ads you like and now see if you can describe what they do differently. Not that easy. And at a £150,000-500,000 entry cost, TV is no cheap hobby! Is it any wonder that online spend has now outstripped traditional broadcast media? Today the internet as a medium offers the prospect everything they need to move on to Step 3. Tell people what you do.

STEP 3 – Facts Match

This step is where most of marketing effort is laid to waste. It is where the previously discussed "Sales Funnel" constricts and narrows. It is where prospects generated by the marketing department are passed to the sales force so that they may get the information they need to purchase. It is the point when warm (emotionally engaged) prospects go cold right there in front of you.

We are all familiar with the constant salesman's bleat: "That lead was no good." Is it the fault of the salesman? Not at all. Is it the fault of the marketing? Shouldn't be.

So who's to blame? Actually no-one. It is simply a failure to understand this key engagement step.

Most sales processes at this point list out the features of the product or service at hand. Take a look your website, your corporate literature, your sales manuals, your exhibition stands.

Admirable lists of features. It's hardly surprising – these pieces of marketing are rarely produced by marketing people working "on" the business but by people working "in" the business. Inevitably they can only describe the value proposition from an internal feature-based perspective.

Consumers use features to deliver the value they think they bought.

Prospects don't buy features, they use them to compare and contrast you to your competition.

In fact you've taken all of the hard work out of getting the information needed to decide how much to value you in comparison to your competitors.

Try it yourself. Go to any electrical retailer and read the product descriptors. Feature-led copy that gives no clue as to which product is best value and is often positively confusing.

No brand relationship will be complete unless you know what the product can do for you. It is also helpful if this is presented in a way that demonstrates how this might differ from other offerings.

So when you tell people what you do, present the **BENEFITS** of your product or service *not* the features.

NOT: If you breakdown our fully qualified roadside engineers are available 24 hours a day.

BUT: Come rain, snow, sun at anytime of the day or night, the AA will come to your rescue in a yellow van driven by a very nice man who'll get you back on the road again.

The Brand Bucket® 1988

You need to establish exactly what you do in a way that is both relevant to the promise from the previous image-match decision step and to what they may actually need to fulfil.

*"What the heart feels today the head will understand
tomorrow"*
Goethe

> **KEY ACTION: At Facts Match you need to introduce the 'Rational' Benefits of your value proposition. These are the 'head' values of your communication campaign.**

Quite clearly, knowing what makes a product good should not be too difficult to establish, and undoubtedly many of those features will be of benefit to the user. The challenge however is to know which ones will influence the purchase decision-making.

The stronger the link to the emotional promise made earlier in Steps 1 and 2, the more likely the customer is going to continue on with their decision-making process. It is no good promising "easy" when the user manual is too complicated to set up the purchase. It is no good offering cheap pricing when there are caveats that make this offer conditional and offputting.

People are not stupid. As David Ogilvy once wrote: "The consumer is not a moron, she is your wife." Whilst in this modern day such a statement might be seen as not politically correct, the point is clear.

We all carry around with us a list of rational expectations against which we mentally audit a sales pitch. You need to be able to understand how these work and how to at least match, or better still exceed, these expectations.

Good salespeople know how to turn features into benefits simply by using their ears and mouth in their respective proportions. By listening, the needs of the prospect are identified and matched by benefits rather than the features.

So far people have become aware, understand how you fit into their lives and what you will do for them. With the right messaging your potential customer should say, **"Now I know who you are and what I'll get from you."**

If they feel that you can complement their image dimensions in a way that will deliver real benefit to them personally then surely those same prospects must now purchase. In many cases this is enough to push them to purchase but research continues to show it often leads to people saying: *"Thank you, when I need you, I will come back."*

And what happens next? Like magic, they disappear. Two key things conspire to generate this response:

1. They may not actually need you at the exact point of time when you are marketing to them, and even if they do, the second point kicks in:

2. You may not be the only choice!

Aha, say the media-owners, you have to keep advertising and generating PR so that when they come back there you are. Simply more waste!

These prospects are already in your Brand Bucket® so why spend money trying to get them back in through the top?

Now you must ensure that the knowledge and desire that the prospect your marketing has created are turned into a memorable experience.

To Step 4.

STEP 4 – Do something together and get a response

The most memorable experience you can give a prospect is by doing something together. An activity where you elicit a direct response from the prospect.

These activities must be motivated by the response:

"I now understand you do exactly what you say you do."

By giving your prospect a first-hand experience of your benefits, they will fully understand the value you will bring to them, and their propensity to part with their hand earned cash will be at its most potent.

In demonstrating how you are in tune with the motivations of the prospect, by offering a "test drive" of your benefits, you will create a new dimension to the relationship that will enhance the quality of life for your prospect and take your value proposition to a whole new level.

The more you interact with your prospect, the more you are **building a stronger relationship** than your competitors who might be selling similar solutions but with whom they have had no interactions. It is imperative that at this stage of the sales process you get people to respond.

Get your prospect to experience the product benefit or at least part of the product benefit.

Each marketing campaign must include an experiential mechanic so that **prospects can directly try out your product.** This is most effective when there is an associated incentive. Whilst this incentive should be in tune with the motivations of the target audience, more importantly, the mechanic must enhance the brand promise and not simply be an "off the shelf" promotional gimmick.

Your **test drive** must create the brand experience in its entirety or at least build a new behavioural pattern that can exclusively belong to you via limited access to your benefits.

The critical factor here is *not* to simply get a response for response's sake. If you do this then your so-called response campaign will really act only as an awareness campaign. Free draws, scratch cards, easy-to-enter competitions are all great things to take part in but unless they are tailored to the brand promise they rarely leave any residual brand value. (Unless of course you are the one who wins the holiday of a lifetime!)

But if you have to buy all your customers a holiday of a lifetime it could work out to be expensive unless the margin on your product is at least £5K. Remember the Hoover promotion? A free flight to New York with every Hoover purchased. Many bought two to get two tickets. They then used one vacuum perhaps whilst the other remained new in the box or appeared on the second hand market at a knock down price.

The promotion went horribly wrong. There were simply not enough flights to meet redemptions. What was worse however was that there was no link between free flights to New York and a Hoover. So the customer experience left no new pattern in the customer's mind that might yield any form of long-term loyalty. That was the real mistake. As a result other competitors were able to capitalise on the vacuum (pun intended).

Whatever your promotion or experiential campaign, it MUST demonstrate the benefits of your product or service that make it special or unique.

This step can be one of the most exciting because it can be the first point of real interaction between you and the prospect but it is often wasted due to lack of work bringing the brand promise to life.

How many exhibitions or shows have you attended where organisations have given away freebie gifts in response to your visiting their stand? How many of them did you keep? How often do you get two things that are the same – stress relief toys, pens, note pads, sweets and mints, and so on? All missed opportunities for those organisations to leave a residual "experience" of their product rather than simply a free gift which gets thrown away later.

Conversely how often have you bought a product after a taste test where you enjoyed the product and chatted with the person who gave you the taste test in the first place? More often that you are prepared to admit I'd bet.

If you do set a pattern in a prospect's mind, if you do raise their expectations, if you do appear to match up to your promise, then a sale is most likely to take place at this point.

Ah, at last, the job of the marketing department is complete.

Actually this is where the job of the marketing really begins! It is where the job of sales ends, often handed over to after-sales or customer relationship managers or the "we've got your money now, leave us alone" department.

This is the time for marketers to really get to work.

It is the time to actually "affect" the full brand experience. A contract has been agreed and paid for between prospect and brand-owner, it is imbued with expectation that must be managed at all times.

Arise all marketers, your time has come.

> **KEY ACTION: Build a 'test drive' into your marketing plan and bring to life those benefits, benefits, benefits.**

STEP 5 – Usage

How often do organisations create a marketing-led aura that simply is not delivered when they come to use the product or service?

This is the real test. Does the product live up to its promise? If it doesn't, you'll have wasted all your previous investment turning the prospect into a consumer. Sure, if all you are interested in is a one-off sale, then getting here is all you need.

However fulfilling consumer expectation is critical to the ongoing relationship between you and the purchaser because those self same people will need far less persuading to buy your product again in the future.

More importantly as trust increases, the less likely they are to be attracted away to your competitors.

Marketing focus on this area allows you to effect simple changes to ensure that you do what you say you do and keep the brand promise alive through every experience. The way a product or service is presented and delivered influences how people feel about their purchase and whether they'll buy your product again.

Every communication opportunity should be used to enhance the product experience, including point of sale materials (POS), packaging, user guides, letters and even contracts and legal documents – in fact, every "touchpoint" of the product or service should be considered as an opportunity for enhancing your value proposition.

> **KEY ACTION: It is critical that the experience of being a customer is included in the marketing plan.**

Take for example the Easter Egg. If you look at the weight of the chocolate that makes up the egg you'll see it is on a par with a small bar of chocolate that you might buy in a confectioner's shop. Yet you pay nearly 10 times the price for it (and in my view the chocolate doesn't even taste as nice). Why are we suckered? For the experience? It comes in the most fantastic wrapper ever. It is an event in itself to open the box. But the experience is short-lived and rarely leaves you in state of long-term satisfaction. Do you always buy the same Easter egg year after year – in fact, have you ever bought the same Easter egg twice (Apart from the ever present cream egg)? Even if you could, then it would be unlikely that the experience ever matches the expectation.

The relationship that results will determine the success or failure of your business. If every time the customer wants to buy again they then have to go in through the top of your Brand Bucket®, the expense to your business will be astronomical. If you become a part of the customer's image dimensions then that cost is hugely reduced.

It is the strength of this relationship that governs people's inclination to purchase. Such relationships ebb and flow and as a result we hold in our heads a list of products, which meet any given need or circumstance. This ladder in the mind is governed by all the brand-influencers and defines who is top.

Think about the last time you went into a sandwich shop. Hunger was the basic need. But what made you walk out with the sandwich you ate in the end? So much to think about, what will you eat at the next meal, do you want spicy or plain, healthy or does it not matter, less than £5 or can I spend more, what drink are you going to have?

At the time it seems a straightforward decision-making process because the brain can handle millions of decisions at any given time but the more you think about what may have influenced that decision about which sandwich to buy the more you realise it is not that simple.

More often than not you will default to a choice that you have made many times before − your regular − because the mind prefers patterns that it recognises when undertaking common activities. Remember how difficult it was to learn to ride a bicycle. Once you have learnt the techniques, no matter when you last rode a bike it seems you can "remember" how to ride.

Brand relationships are no different and the challenge for marketing communication is to break through some of these "remembered" patterns and establish new ones. It is not easy to replace existing patterns so that your product becomes the preferred one.

This step is where the full meaning of "brand" as defined earlier comes into play. Marketing must be used to affect the relationship building and reinforce the patterns in the mind at all times.

Get this right and you will have attained the most valuable asset a business can have and one that smart marketers should put at the top of the list. This asset sits at the bottom of The Brand Bucket®.

STEP 6 – Loyalty

Or: creating the most valued asset in your business.

If your customer has made it this deep into your Brand Bucket® they've become your most valuable asset for three reasons.

1. They've cost you a lot to get them there.
2. As loyal users of your product they have the potential to become advocates, your most valuable marketing tool, working on your behalf to direct new customers into the bucket.
3. If you don't look after them they'll become potential barriers to the purchasing process for others.

Think of your own experiences. How often have you gone through a process not dissimilar to the five steps described above only to find yourself totally ignored or treated to an "off the shelf" aftercare package? The chances are that you will become disenchanted very quickly and probably not buy the product again let alone recommend the product to somebody else.

And yet you are the most valuable asset a business can have. You are its brand custodian and even better still, you will probably tell others how good the brand can be for them.

A well marketed business ensures that these people are consulted, heard and looked after accordingly.

They then become the brand powerhouse, they are the loyalists.

But beware, they come in 4 different guises:

1. There are those who, in signing up to your brand story, would seek to claim a seat on the Board and want to know what you are up to all the time.

2. Equally there are those who will happily use your product for ever, just don't change it and under no circumstances try and sell them anything else.

3. There are those who simply bought into your offer at the time because it met their immediate Brand Bucket® requirements and will be loyal until something better engages them.

4. There are those who just bought on price and will only stay as long as you remain the cheapest.

Most people fall into one or other of these categories all the time. Lack of effort here by the brand-owner and all can be lost in an instant, especially with the way technology is used today. You are one negative blog, one penetration pricing strategy, one breakdown, one bad experience away from having a massive hole in your bucket.

It is imperative that loyalists have their own special place on your marketing plan. The age-old adage that for many businesses 80% of custom comes from only 20% of their customers is still as true as it ever was. **This is no time to ignore this 80:20 rule.**

Because of the journey you have taken your customer through and the fact that they have entered into a valued relationship with you, these customers see you as very much part of their own image dimensions, how they see themselves.

You need to reinforce the impression that you value their custom by talking with them all the time.

Demonstrate understanding of what they must be going through and how they can continually benefit from your product or service and they will never leave you. Parting company with your brand means your consumer has to become a prospect again. Going through someone else's Brand Bucket® and finding an alternative adds additional risk to how they see themselves.

Focus on this area and don't be surprised if they go and tell everyone about you and how good you are.

Advocacy should be a marketing goal rather than simply a justification of a business-owner's ego.

> **KEY ACTION: Look after those most valued, they might well look after you !**

Marketing plans that are based on the 6 steps outlined are the most successful in generating sales because the prospect is managed throughout their decision-making process, and even after they have become consumers, continuous marketing effort keeps them in The Brand Bucket®.

5

WHY SHOULD YOUR MARKETING PLAN BE BUCKET-SHAPED?

Since its inception, The Brand Bucket® has been tested directly by brand-owners and Marketing Directors all over the world across almost every sector you could possibly associate with marketing.

Although originated for a car manufacturer it has been subsequently applied to make marketing work for Fast Moving Consumer Goods (FMCG); White and Brown Goods; Not for Profit companies and Charities; property; technology; business services; professional services; lawyers and accountants; start ups; fashion; retail; online and offline FTSE and NASDAQ listed companies. The list of brands, products and services that have been touched by The Brand Bucket® is extensive.

All have reported back whether anecdotally, through quantitative research (number-based research) or qualitative research (opinion-based research) that the application of the 6 steps leads to a bucket shape.

If you look at the response figures at each level of The Brand Bucket®, you will always find that no matter what the product or service, there are always more prospects who have heard of you than customers who actually use you regularly.

There is a clear relationship between the first step where there are the largest number of people and each diminishing step until the final 6th step where there are likely to be least of all.

As people experience your value proposition and move through various decision-making steps a proportion, often for very practical reasons, will decide not to progress with your particular brand relationship.

For example:

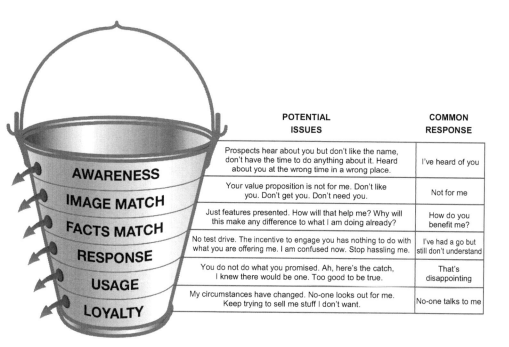

	POTENTIAL ISSUES	COMMON RESPONSE
AWARENESS	Prospects hear about you but don't like the name, don't have the time to do anything about it. Heard about you at the wrong time in a wrong place.	I've heard of you
IMAGE MATCH	Your value proposition is not for me. Don't like you. Don't get you. Don't need you.	Not for me
FACTS MATCH	Just features presented. How will that help me? Why will this make any difference to what I am doing already?	How do you benefit me?
RESPONSE	No test drive. The incentive to engage you has nothing to do with what you are offering me. I am confused now. Stop hassling me.	I've had a go but still don't understand
USAGE	You do not do what you promised. Ah, here's the catch, I knew there would be one. Too good to be true.	That's disappointing
LOYALTY	My circumstances have changed. No-one looks out for me. Keep trying to sell me stuff I don't want.	No-one talks to me

These are a sample of some of the common reasons people leak out of the bucket at each level. There are literally thousands of reasons.

A well marketed business will see these and have a plan that can nimbly adjust to plug the leaks and keep more people in The Brand Bucket®.

Constant monitoring of the acquisition process often yields these areas of leakage. If you get salespeople talking to marketing people, talking to product developers, talking to business-owners and shareholders, you'll be amazed how many potential areas for leakage can be blocked up very quickly.

The numbers support this qualitative approach too.

Take for example the formula for a successful Google Adwords campaign.

Awareness = Impressions

The number of people who key in your chosen keyword and have the opportunity to see your Adword ad under "sponsored links" at the top or to the right hand side of your search results.

Image Match = Your Adwords Ad

The use of three lines to make your offer appear consisting of the title line and two description lines and web address. Written well, (it has to be because you are restricted to 25:35:35 characters on each line) this ad should appeal to only a proportion of your impressions who will click on your ad to go to your website. (This is when you pay Google.)

Facts Match = The Landing Page On Your Website

Send them to your website home page and make them work out how they can benefit from your product or service and they will disappear in droves (called "bounce rate" by Google). Create a landing page specific to the Brand Bucket® relationship generated by the keyword and click through.

Response = Capture their contact details

If the only way to get more information is to complete a five-minute online form, including data they may not even have to hand, this is a sure fine way to punch a hole in your bucket.

Keep data capture simple and exchange their effort for a little of yours. A free report, gift, seminar or site visit or online quote are all examples of effort on your part. Make it something you'd personally leave your own details for!

Response = Manage Expectations

Asking them to pay now, call a personal representative or sign up are all ways to lose a prospect. No credit card to hand, can't find the relevant contact details to call, or a sign-up process that is so arduous you need a degree in English and computer science to complete it, are all barriers to moving to the next step – purchase!

Loyalty = Automating the responses

"Thank you for giving us your money" system-generated emails are great for the business-owner but often provide little reassurance for the new customer. **An automated response does not mean automated thinking.** When was the last time you reviewed your automated response procedure, your welcome letters, etc.?

This can be a great opportunity to lock in your new consumers and even get more prospects into the top of your bucket with a "recommend a friend" incentive.

It is worth noting that according to Gallup the leaks you can do little about are lost consumers through death (1%) and move-aways (4%) every year. If you do nothing you'll lose 5% of your consumer base. How long before this becomes critical?

No matter what approach you take to marketing your business, the top of your bucket **(X)** is always wider than the bottom **(Y)**.

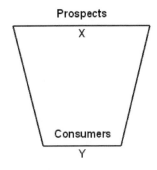

Prospects

X

Consumers

Y

However, the **success of your marketing** or indeed your business is **NOT the size of the top of your bucket** but how wide it is at the bottom. The more successful your marketing using The Brand Bucket®, the smaller the ratio is between **X : Y**.

In putting a marketing plan together, nobody should start at the top of the bucket and work their way down.

"Let's see what we can afford and allocate a marketing budget."

A recipe for waste because unavoidably the top of The Brand Bucket® involves giving money to other companies, media-owners, printers, consultants whose main interest is to wrestle your marketing budget from you! Again not the fault of the media-owner or the fault of the advertising agent. Their business model does not allow any other form of thinking. They simply know no different.

By starting at the bottom of The Brand Bucket® you are in full control over how your marketing spend feeds directly into your business plan. Ask these simple questions first:

🪣 How many consumers do we want?
🪣 What are they worth to us?

Then work your way up The Brand Bucket® from there.

The following formula can act as a guide:

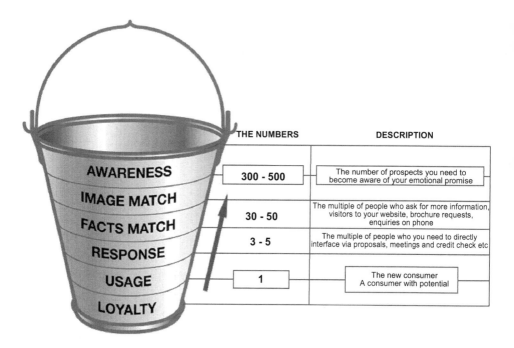

THE NUMBERS		DESCRIPTION
AWARENESS	300 - 500	The number of prospects you need to become aware of your emotional promise
IMAGE MATCH	30 - 50	The multiple of people who ask for more information, visitors to your website, brochure requests, enquiries on phone
FACTS MATCH	3 - 5	The multiple of people who you need to directly interface via proposals, meetings and credit check etc
RESPONSE		
USAGE	1	The new consumer A consumer with potential
LOYALTY		

The above represents a good starting point for any marketing plan. The idea is improve on these metrics.

By improving your conversion ratio from 5 to 3 your cost savings at awareness/image building can be as much as 50%.

6

FEW BUSINESSES HAVE A PERFECT BUCKET SHAPE

If you have begun to think about your business in terms of The Brand Bucket®, you will undoubtedly soon realise that you do not have a perfect bucket shape.

In fact, you may not have a bucket shape at all. Do not despair, very few businesses do, and, almost without exception, all businesses fall into one of three other shapes only: a funnel shape, an hourglass shape and a terrarium shape.

By understanding the shape into which your brand relationship falls, you can quickly and cost-effectively adjust your marketing activity to ensure there is a flow from the top of the bucket into the bottom.

In the world of Marketing Speak, there is often a reference to a "sales pipe" and were this to exist, this book would be redundant as this would be the perfect sales and marketing solution.

Every prospect becomes a customer.

Now that would be good. Unfortunately, only two things have ever been identified as having a pipe shape: death and taxes, both of which are unavoidable!

Let us consider each of the three non-bucket shapes in turn:

The Funnel Brand Shape

This brand shape occurs when there are high levels of awareness and an established image amongst the target audience but this has simply not translated into tangible sales.

Back in the land of Marketing Speak people often refer to the marketing or sales funnel. The existence of this funnel is a longstanding misconception related to the sales process.

Try holding a funnel and pouring water into it (cf prospects). How many customers do you catch? Not many and you'll probably end up with wet feet.

For a funnel to be effective, it must be placed into another receptacle.

And here lies the problem with many businesses with separate sales and marketing operations. They all too often assume (defined as making an "ass" out of "u" and "me") that the business will be geared to accepting sales leads and have in place conversion programmes tailored to the nature and type of sales leads coming in.

And yet an all-too-common board meeting question remains: **Why are there not enough sales?**

This brand shape is characterised by marketing which has successfully opened up the top of The Brand Bucket® creating a funnel but the decision-making process is breaking as the prospect tries to decipher what the benefits are for them.

If that search takes too long then the chances are that with heightened interest the prospect is looking at alternatives to your offer, giving your competitors an opportunity to jump in and effectively steal your prospect.

Advertising takes the brunt of criticism when this shape is apparent. Not surprising given that very few ad campaigns can deliver more than awareness and image dimensions. It's often expensive too.

The main reason for this is most likely to be that in creating this fantastic awareness and image the marketing plan quite simply neglects to include steps to tell people how the product or service will actually benefit them. Try watching the commercials on TV one night. There will be many approaches to the use of the airtime seconds.

Each business will have created a way of getting you to feel something about them but can you really explain what it is they do differently.

Start with insurance advertising! Or Banks. Cars or perfumes. Shampoos or...or...

The solution is often much simpler than you might think. Inject the marketing plan with campaigns that clearly tell people how you will benefit them and incentivise a test drive of one or all of these benefits – get more people to use your products and services as part of their everyday lifestyle.

Funnel case study: E✱TRADE

In 1997 no-one had really heard of "online" trading here in the UK, but in the US they were already developing mainstream brands in this category. One such brand was E*Trade, which was at one stage to become the world's number one online broker. (Thanks in part to The Brand Bucket® in 1996.)

News soon spread through the "in-the-know" financial community of the presence of E*Trade and how a Vietnam veteran, Christos Cotsakos, was putting fear into the hearts of the traditional brokerage industry.

Having used The Brand Bucket® to grow from 200,000 customers to around 3 million in the US, E*Trade decided to launch the brand in the UK.

Precursory research amongst the early adopters of online broking showed that E*Trade had sufficient awareness in the UK amongst this select group and that a highly targeted facts-match trial campaign, through the financial press, was required.

Launching in 1998, E*Trade became the best known born-on-the-net brokerage brand within 6 months – winning the most awards for their site design and user-friendliness at the much coveted *Investors' Chronicle* Awards.

The Brand Bucket® was used to provide the whole communication strategy as well as the collateral to fulfil its promise, including application forms, Internet and DM promotions, mouse mats and give-aways, exhibition stands, lead kits and start-up guides.

The starting point was to understand what underpinned the awareness and image and to draw that down The Brand Bucket® throughout the marketing mix. In this way the top fed into the bottom. To enable this, the logo became the hero of the brand architecture by integrating their "converging purple and green arrows" icon into all the communication. Using the two strong colours throughout, and more importantly creating a tone of voice that was both unique to the broker market as well as being a key differentiator, meant that none of the competitors could match them because, like Schwab and JDS, for example, they all had traditional broker arms to their business.

In only 24 months E*Trade were able to boast in the region of 25,000 customers.

The Hourglass Brand Shape

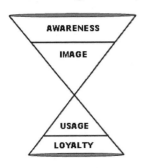

The second shape that characterises many businesses is the hourglass where a business has good awareness amongst its prospects, a reasonable Image Match with that audience and a good collection of customers who are more than happy with the product or service. And yet there is an underlying problem with the business itself.

Sales seem static or may even be showing a slight decay.

What this suggests is that there is a mismatch between the

top and the bottom of the bucket with people coming in at Awareness and Image and not making it down to Usage and Loyalty.

There are a number of possible reasons for this:

1. The people coming in at in the top are the wrong kind of people. Broadcast marketing is bringing plenty of people into the bucket who very quickly say "not for me".

2. The prospects are the right people but the image being conveyed by the brand is not in line with their emotional needs.

3. The people at the bottom of the bucket are there for the reasons that are not fully understood or once had been true of your business offer but have now changed.

4. Most commonly it is simply because your prospects don't get it. They have not understood how you are going to benefit them.

The solution is broadly the same for all the above scenarios. First talk to your existing customers and get a clear understanding of why they buy from you. Find out from them how they think you benefit them. Then take this information and match it against what people at the top of the bucket are expecting to get from you.

There is certain to be a discrepancy between the two. You then have the choice of changing your image at the top of the bucket or changing the way you work at the bottom amongst loyalists.

The challenge is to do this without alienating either group because they are hard-earned. If you seek to change the top, this must be linked through to the bottom with a clear communication strategy at the Facts Match and Response steps.

Case study: Lucozade

In the 80s Lucozade confronted a real problem. As a long established brand, Lucozade was well known but for being a pleasant pick-me-up drink when you were ill. The brand was seen as almost medicinal in image. That, combined with the fact that the supermarkets were beginning to really take a hold as a dominant route to market and in turn wanted more shelf space for a whole host of new soft drinks entering the market at the time, placed real pressure on the big glass bottle with the cellophane wrapper.

But there were a significant number of drinkers who drank Lucozade regularly simply because they liked the taste. They drank it even though they were not ill.

Lucozade undertook a large Usage & Awareness (U&A) study and a programme of taste test studies and from these identified that younger people liked the product but would never consider it in their soft drink repertoire because the brand was perceived as old-fashioned. Its medicinal image elicited the familiar response "I only drink this when I'm ill."

As a result the top of the bucket had been opened in a way that presented the brand as "restorative" and this was fully endorsed by those who were loyal to the brand.

The challenge was to change beliefs surrounding the brand without alienating the existing customer base. In business terms this group were too valuable to risk losing overnight even though they were slowly decreasing in value terms.

A single consumer insight driven key message was identified and consistently driven through all brand

relationship marketing – ENERGY.

The result was a repositioning of Lucozade through the use of Daly Thompson, a gold medal Olympic decathlon athlete who drank it whilst training to aid recovery![1] This was supported by a series of award-winning posters featuring a giant NRG.

The product itself was repackaged into small stubbie bottles and squashy bags designed to provide the perfect intake of fluid.

The distribution was specifically channelled to aid the belief structure of the brand with the sale of the product though gyms and tennis clubs. This had the added

---

[1] A task indeed to convince the then ITVA (Independent Television Authority) – now the BACC (British Advertising Clearance Committee) – television approval authorities.

advantage of growing the distribution without affecting the existing distribution channels through the supermarkets.

Key to the strategy was providing trial opportunities through promotions that fed the new positioning, such as taste promotions at major sporting events. Plus Lucozade sponsored the large squeezy bottles for football players to get additional fluids during football matches. (An idea inspired by Gatorade in the US.)

Very soon the bottom of the bucket began to fill with a whole new set of drinkers who came to the brand with its new positioning. What was more exciting was that the erosion of the older customer base was not as dramatic as had been feared because the "energy lift" message was consistent with what they believed about the product anyway.

Finally, Lucozade's product extension strategy was brought into line with the overall communication strategy through the introduction of the sport-orientated "isotonic" still range.

Today Lucozade is seen as very much a mainstream sports drink and can be found in coolers throughout in Confectioners Tobacconists and Newsagents (CTNs) in the UK and still enjoys a place on the supermarket shelves.

The Terrarium Brand Shape

The third shape is the terrarium. Plant growers will be familiar with this old glass bottle, once familiar to the cider lover but now more commonly used as a perfect microclimate for various forms of greenery. Carefully nurtured, these plants grow healthily and fill up the bottle.

Many businesses establish themselves this same way. They spend considerable time building healthy customer-centric relationships and believe they are creating a strong business but for some reason the number of customers remain static or, again, may even be in decline. And yet the business offer is very much appreciated by the existing customer base, so the picture within the business is often misleading or confusing at board level.

"Why is it that our customers are happy but prospects fail to be attracted to the business?"

This shape is one of the most common shapes for businesses. Lots of happy customers but increasingly more difficult to get new ones. Quite some conundrum, a running business with good products or services. Efforts, if any, are put into sales and marketing, but still leave the business stagnant or worse still, just seeing profit erosion. (Probably thanks to all that broadcast marketing!)

Most of the focus of the business has been on providing better value for the existing consumers, something that customer feedback consistently supports. But there are few if any new prospects widening the top of The Brand Bucket®.

More often than not the business has tried broadcast marketing through consultants and, if not, has tried marketing on their own – "well any fool can do that!"

The net outcome of this is that the advertising probably hasn't yielded the results that were anticipated. Again this is not surprising because the chances are that although your target market have seen the ad they have found little opportunity to do much about it other than take the list of features and use these as a shopping list to compare you to your competitors.

Even if you are better than them, there is a good chance that the sales process suffers from the fact before a final decision can be made there needs to be a search to see if there is something better out there. And as the search continues there is a delay in making that final decision leading to the whole purchase cycle breaking down.

By then your advertising is probably long forgotten just as you are getting the bills for it!

The principle of such campaigns is not in question here; it is simply that the thinking and therefore the messaging in the campaign has only risen from the bottom of The Brand Bucket® up as high as Facts Match resulting in communications that do little more than convey the features of the business.

Remember working "in" the business vs working "on" the business?

The advantage of having the terrarium shape is that you already have a reliable source of information about how your business benefits people. Just ask your staff and your current consumers. They will willingly reveal what makes your offer special.

With this information to hand you can package it in a way that will be enticing for your prospects coming through the top of the bucket.

Case Study: SAAB

In 1984 SAAB were seeking to move into the mainstream of car manufacturing in the UK and wanted to understand how people bought motor cars. After commissioning a large piece of research into how people bought motor cars, the result was the Brand Bucket® methodology now becoming clearer to you.

When the perceptions of the SAAB brand were first evaluated against The Brand Bucket® it was immediately clear that SAAB had a very distinctive terrarium shape. Existing SAAB owners were not only passionate about their car but verged on the almost evangelical. And yet those who did not drive a SAAB remained almost entirely in the dark about why you should own a SAAB. The challenge was to find the key to this evangelism – and as is often the case, the answer lay in the product itself.

SAAB stood for Svenska Aeroplan AktieBolaget and this Swedish aircraft manufacturer was responsible for the design and build of the Viggen fighter plane.

The experience of driving a SAAB 900 was inspired by the experience of piloting this fighter plane, with the driver at the very heart of the SAAB driving experience. The interior of the vehicle was treated like a cockpit, the engine given "take-off" credentials, the handling response was immediate, the breaking system exceptional. If a car could fly then your SAAB was as close as you could get.

The result was a straight analogy between aircraft and car, and pilot and driver, leading to the award-winning commercials featuring a car racing a Viggen fighter plane. Okay, so the plane wins but the point is well made.

By portraying SAAB in this way, and they still do it today, as prospects moved through the 6 steps their experience matched the expectation set up at the top of the bucket and evangelism was assured.

7

MAKING YOUR MARKETING WORK – WHAT SHAPE IS YOUR BUSINESS IN?

Now is the time to run The Brand Bucket® analysis over your business. Taking time out to do this will save hours of meetings with colleagues, staff and consultants.

It will give you a shape to indicate how your brand communication is working at the moment and give you a real sense of where you can place emphasis to make sure your marketing is effective – and more importantly, identify areas where a little effort can produce almost instantaneous results. The act of undertaking the exercise will provide a roadmap for the journey that if followed will get you to destination sales.

Who is your ideal prospect?

The first exercise is to write a short narrative as described in Chapter 3 to identify your ideal prospect from a psychographic point of view. This is the potential buyer of your service.

If you can, give them a name like Mavericks or Mr Analytical or Mrs Gamer. This will act as a short hand when revisiting how your marketing works.

The temptation will be to say you have hundreds of different types of prospects so how can you define them all into one? No matter how big the brand, rarely are there more than three profiles required as long as you stick to a psychographic description. Keep it simple. It should be no more than one half page for each profile.

If you ask your sales staff and your customer service staff to describe the perfect customer you'll soon see a pattern emerge and if you capture the consistent elements it will make creating the brand conversation much easier. You will then know who you are talking to for a start, and therefore engaging them should be made much easier.

Now set your sales target

Before you start fretting about how your marketing is working, it is imperative you decide how many consumers of your product or service you want, need, or more often than not, can cope with.

This number provides the context for judging whether your marketing is successful. Your business plan should tell you this. If you haven't got one, then get one. It doesn't have to be a 60-page thesis for the bank. A simple one-page one is good enough. The numbers of customers you want should be captured by specific Key Performance Indicators (KPI's) which link directly to your one number: **the amount of money you want to make after tax!**

Without your one number and sales targets, all your marketing effort will be like whistling in the wind. (Sounds good close by but can't be heard 10ft away.)

Again these need only be simple statements of intent: 12 months worth of sales by product or service, by highest margin and lowest margin, by distributor, online/offline sales.

In no time you'll have a mini plan before you that everyone can work towards achieving.

As you run your marketing you should check daily against your one-page business map to see if your efforts are having the right effect.

Business is a numbers game. By starting with the one number you can work back through the product set and identify where you should be focusing your marketing effort to glean the most profit.

Only this is the true barometer of whether your value proposition has actual value.

Now you are very close to creating a one-page marketing plan for the business. There is one missing piece to make your marketing work. **The Value Proposition.**

Starting in the right place

Getting your value proposition in place is the most fundamental thing you need for successful marketing. Gut instinct will simply not do. You cannot build a house without firm foundations so attempting to build a strong relationship with your prospects and consumers without a clear brand story is just plain stupid.

The ultimate value proposition feeds the Brand Bucket® 6 Steps from within the business. To stop a bucket rusting and springing leaks you need to galvanise the metal from the inside!

A brand relationship is no different so you need **The Brand Galvaniser™** a representation of the aerial view into your Brand Bucket®.

The Brand Galvaniser™

Your brand story feeds almost everything that comes from your business. It is the inner drive for the value that your prospects and your consumers will buy from you.

Unfortunately like all important things this is probably the hardest part of developing marketing that will work. The creation of a story that other people want to buy from you is almost **impossible when you are working *in* the business** because you can only do it if you work *on* the business.

The obvious thing to do is to ask those who do buy from you *why* they do. Unfortunately their expectations are entirely governed by a form of "contract" because they parted with a payment, money or otherwise. The result is that the relationship is already equalised out with both parties looking to leverage the relationship in their favour. Profit versus experience.

This tension will not give an accurate story that prospects will find entirely convincing.

It is of course great if you only want to sell to existing customers but in real terms this will limit the growth of your business unless your consumers have clones.

This leaves asking people unrelated to your business to tell you what they would want from you. No again. In the end, they can only give you their impression of what you offer, based on their own personal perception.

So if you can't ask the people who might buy from you or ask those who do buy from you and you can't ask people inside your business who do you ask? Not an easy conundrum and probably why most businesses don't have a defined value proposition.

The following approach will take you a long way down the path but in the end you will need a close friend or business advisor who has a marketing background to steer you across the finishing line. You might even ask your marketing agency, if you have one, to give you a hand. The key to unlocking this story lies with them, but the treasure trove that is behind the lock lies with you!

Many companies ask for external help and end up with a set of so-called "brand guidelines". If you have ever read any of these you will have realised that these are not brand guidelines at all. They are often simply rules for the use of your logo and look and feel. They are one of the most expensive pieces of shelfware you'll ever buy.

Often these "brand guidelines" contain a plethora of feeble mechanics that the originating agency has put in place to help you with your value proposition: Mission Statements; Positioning Statements; our 6 key words; what photos we use; our font style; our tagline; logo exclusion zones.

All of these are meant to enable a business to brand themselves. Now if you accept the earlier premise that a brand is in fact a relationship then these tools should be about "affecting" that relationship and with this in mind, very quickly, you'll see this is simply not the case. The target market for brand guidelines is rarely the prospects, might be existing consumers, but is most likely the people working in the business or worse still, the board or the person paying the bill.

Actually if you are serious about marketing then they are often an insult to a business-owner's intelligence. No wonder paying thousands of pounds for a ten-page booklet with brand guidelines written on the front is so painful.

The answer is to use a representative of both parties involved in building this all-important valued relationship. You and someone external to you with the expertise to convert your "in" the business viewpoint into an "on" the business viewpoint.

Back to your value proposition. There are four key elements that make up your value proposition:

- How your brand behaves
- What do you do for people
- What should consumers believe about you
- A statement of intent: the what, why and for whom of your business that you can do differently.

1. How your brand behaves

This section of your value proposition feeds the first two steps of The Brand Bucket® underpinning both Awareness and Image. The values you list here will set the tone of your brand, what it is like to communicate with you and how you are going to complement the personal values of your prospects.

Think about your business, product or service as a person. How would you describe them? Simply listing out all of the values of your business will give you a context into which you can place all your marketing. Scan the whole offer from initial contact right through to after sales.

Different values will prevail at different times. Most brands have between 20 and 30 behavioural traits. Often these can appear to be opposites. Think tears of a clown.

Comedians are often not funny at all off stage (especially when they don't get paid). Businesses are no different. Being approachable doesn't prevent you being driven, precise, or demanding (that's the money thing again). Think about your bank. The joviality of your bank manager on the squash court or down the golf club is not what you want when you want him to handle your money! (Actually don't think about your bank manager, few have covered themselves in glory in recent times.)

Try listing them out on separate pieces of paper. It takes about 20 minutes and a good cup of coffee or tea.

This list represents all the behavioural traits of your organisation. Be amazed when you start to see your staff as representations of these traits and how they differ in different departments. Accounts versus front desk; shop floor versus warehouse; canteen versus product development. Each trait has an important role to play and handled correctly can be orientated towards a wide range of marketing traits amongst your prospects and customers.

2. What you do for people

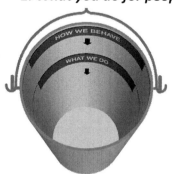

The section of your value proposition is the most important because is the repository of all your benefits, the things prospects buy from you. These benefits will drive your communication messaging throughout your marketing. Get these right and people will give you money! Most business-owners, when asked what they do, quickly, confidently and easily list out features of their business. Great if you are a consumer – the more features the better – but a total turn-off for a prospect. At best they will overcome their boredom by using your features list to compare you to the competition to see who comes out on top. Features listings are the preserve of the owner of the product or service not the person thinking of buying.

The only true question is **what do you do for people?**

In other words what would they understand to be a benefit of your business offer, your product or your service.

Now this is really hard for any business-owner because they are only able to see features and rarely, if ever, benefits. Try it now. Another cuppa to hand, (you may need something stronger), write down all the benefits you offer.

Just to get you going here are some benefits that aren't benefits at all:

1F Saves time and money................ Feature
2F Open 24 hours a day.................. Feature
3F Eat as much as you like.............. Feature
4F Families welcome....................... Feature
5F Full money back guarantee........ Feature

Of course they all have benefits *behind* them, but as a prospect you have still to decide what these might be and if the perceived benefit is sufficiently motivating to differentiate the brand feature over someone else's. If you are not sure, read your own website. Guaranteed to be packed with features of your business!

A benefit is something that when read elicits the response **"I want to own that"**, whether it is something intellectual or physical.

Let's try again and see if we can convert the features above into a benefit:

1B Spend more free time with the family.......... Benefit
2B We're always here for you............................. Benefit
3B Tummy satisfaction guaranteed..................... Benefit
4B We take care of children too......................... Benefit
5B Full refund if it doesn't do what you want ... Benefit

Ideally you should list out up to 20 benefits for your business offer. Probably time to ask a friend. Your chosen business advisor can listen to your benefits and advise if they really feel like benefits. If they do, **lock them in**. If they sound like features role-play until they are reworded as benefits.

It really is worth the effort. The more there are, the more meaningful they are, and the more likely people will find them appealing and spend money on your brand!

Not everyone will value each benefit the same but now you have the tools to underpin your Facts Match and your Response "test drives".

3. What consumers should believe about you

That leaves us with Usage and Loyalty.

A successful value proposition must leave you in no doubt as to how to make your marketing work and one of the best tools for this is to create a way of judging if your message hits the mark.

The way to do this is by starting with what you want people to believe once they have been engaged by you. If you want to be famous for the colour red (Coca-Cola) then using blue (Pepsi) is a real risk. The commitment to owning the colour red changed Santa Claus forever.[2] Now this may be an over simplification but

the point is key. If you want to be seen as always there for the consumer, make sure your marketing promises that. If you want to be my best friend, demonstrate how you are going to be my best friend always.

Marketers call this "consumer take-out".

It is simply what you want people to believe about you after they have interacted with you at every level of The Brand Bucket®.

---

[2] It is commonly believed that Coca Cola turned Santa red but the red colour was in fact introduced by Thomas Nast during the 30 years that he drew Santa for Harpers Weekly between 1869 -1900. Coca Cola Santa advertising did not start until 1922.

4. Bringing it all together

You now have no more than 20 words to capture the outer rings in one statement. This is your statement of intent, **the differentiating core** to your brand.

Your intent to create a differentiated relationship that people will value over all others.

It's a statement of "will you marry me?" The answer *"yes"* is met with a sale. The answer *"no"* spells a start-over for both parties. This differentiated core statement is a promise from you the business-owner to the person you love most, a promise to deliver valuable product or service, a promise to make a difference for the lifetime of the relationship.

A toilet roll has a value proposition in the same way as a car, a holiday company or a political party. All are brands.

Now it would be great to say in the world of texting, Facebook and Twitter that these 20 words are easy to write. Conveying ideas in these media continues to prove that this remains a skill that few have mastered. (The quality of literacy and thought too often leaves much to be desired. This is a skill that is still to be found amongst the headline writers in the broadcast media and their complementary advertising agencies. May they emerge intact and embrace social networking online. It needs it).

For the meantime the pressure is on you to write those 20 words because it is from your differentiating core that all of your marketing will flow.

The key to your differentiating core, your statement of intent is that it must encompass three elements:

1. Your ideal prospect and therefore consumer
2. What you will provide
3. What is the ultimate benefit.

Only six words for each area and when you match all of the words and phrases to your differentiating core, they should all work together.

Some example statements of intent:

Marie Curie Cancer Care provides high quality nursing, totally free, to give terminally ill people the choice of dying at home, supported by their families.

With E*Trade you have the power to take control of your investments.

Thinking optical solutions

Bookham Technology leads the way with optical solutions that deliver real customer benefit.

Once you have all the core material you can complete your very own Brand Galvaniser™:

Auditing your own brand

With your perfect prospect profile to hand and having established how many of them you want, and with your value proposition captured in your very own Brand Galvaniser™, you are now ready to analyse how well your engagement strategy is working.

Start at the top of your Brand Bucket®.

1. Awareness

The most common mistake here is to try and identify how well known you are in the marketplace – what's your coverage; let's get the name out there. Sure if people haven't heard of you they are unlikely to consider you but we now also a have a damn good idea of how many people we need to get to hear of us to meet our sales targets using the metric formula described in chapter 5.

Based on that, if you want to attract ten new clients, then you only need 3,000 people to have heard of you.

If you want to sell 1,000 products a day, you only need

500,000 people to have heard of you. Why then do you need a broadcast campaign that gets you more? That is wasteful.

There are other contributors to how successful you are at building awareness. The name of the product or service can really help the propensity to engage. Again with a combination of your Value Proposition and your psychographic target profile to hand you can easily judge for example whether Tinky Winky, Dipsy, LaLa and Po are good names for a Law Firm.

Your naming strategy will affect your marketing plan because different levels of engagement require different marketing approaches:

Name Type	Example	Marketing requirement
Descriptive	Toys R Us, Kwik-fit, E*Trade	Need personality added as offer is very rational.
Personality-led	Jack Daniels, Ben & Jerry's, Boots, Marks & Spencer, Sainsbury's, Ford	Need to more information to convey how these brands reflect the values of the founder.
Coded	WPP (Wire and Plastic Products – shopping trolleys to you and me) IBM (International Business Machines) BP (British Petroleum) BT (British Telecom)	These names are designed to hide their origin as the interpretation of this might be detrimental to the brand promise so new meaning can be added easily.
Made up names	Accenture, Google, Yahoo, Occado, Aviva	Often newer brands to market need to find a domain name that isn't taken and try to reflect what the company does. Marketing needs to explain what they represent and more effort needed to explain the brand promise.
Iconic names	Shell, Coca Cola, McDonalds, SKY, Apple, Nike	These names lead their marketing through ownership of an icon which lives at every level of the brand experience.

This is by no means exhaustive but demonstrates how each and every naming strategy requires a different marketing approach.

With a sense of how much *"I've heard of you"* you have in place in your business it is time to look at your Image Match dimensions.

2. Image Match

If you review all the imagery that you use in your business you'll soon get a feeling for how much of your marketing elicits the "I

see where you fit into my life" response.

Start with the overall look and feel of your communication. Consider everything in your business. The cups in the canteen, the uniform the staff wear, the signs in the car park, the noticeboard, the email sign off, your business cards, your meeting room.

The internal reflection of your business will be a good indication of what is appearing in your brochures, your ads and on your website.

Can the people who come into contact with your business – whether daily as employees or regularly as suppliers or distributors or infrequently as prospects and consumers – immediately get the feeling you want to convey?

Everything must reflect the essence of your value proposition. Good copy and design can do this and

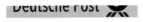

by placing a strong hint of it at every brand touchpoint it will help bring everything together.

A picture really can say a thousand words; a good design property can do the same. It acts to remind, it acts to endorse, it acts as a signpost to let the target know where they are at all times. Most of all, it reassures, through a mark of quality. It makes people feel secure in the knowledge that it's for them.

By making sure your marketing makes people feel good about themselves, then they will align with your brand more readily than the competition.

A quick test is the tagline you have with your logo. Is it a descriptor? Or is it this is how we make a difference to your quality of life statement?

Avoid the naming trap here. For example,

J. Smith & Sons. Painters and Decorators.

Because the name can't tell us what the business does, the line has been written to do so. As a prospect there is no reason or desire to use this firm over and above any other painter and decorator.

It would work better as:

J. Smith & Sons. Making interiors and exteriors more beautiful.

By now there should be a sense of how wide open the top of your Brand Bucket® is in real terms. If it's not that wide or not open enough, the work must start here. If you are happy that there are enough prospects pouring into your bucket then it's time to make sure the next step is working well.

3. Facts Match

Getting people to part with their hard-earned cash really starts here because this is where having got them to have heard of you (and like you) they now start to work out if what you are offering is of value to them – and if so, is it worth more than the money in their pocket?

The approach here must service the "what's in it for me" attitude of the prospect, so everything you communicate at this point of the decision-making process must convey the benefit.

> *People don't want a 10mm drill but they want a 10mm hole*
>
> *People don't want a 3 hour flight, they want the fastest way to get to a destination*
>
> *People don't want a filled sandwich, they want something tasty to fill them up*

If you leave a prospect to work out the benefit for themselves, then you run the risk of them giving up and going somewhere else before they have worked it out or, more costly to you, working out a benefit which you may not even offer, ensuring disappointment later on invariably at your expense!

KEY ACTION: Review all of your messaging everywhere.

A visit to Port Sunlight near Liverpool, the heart of Unilever cleaning product manufacture, built by Lord Leverhulme himself, was a touch undermined when it was discovered that the contractor employed to clean the toilets was using Procter and Gamble products to do so!

Leave no stone unturned.

From a marketing perspective every possible opportunity to convey the benefits must be taken.

Review your reception; your proposals; your contracts;

packaging; email sign-offs; website; brochure; letters and faxes. Without too much effort a picture will emerge as to whether you are getting your value proposition across at every opportunity.

Don't be surprised if this area is not strong in your business. It will undoubtedly feel like this should be the easiest part but experience shows that it is human nature when you are working "in" the business to take the good parts for granted.

The mind logs what it likes and parks the good things away into a pattern in the brain that we all take for granted. Disturb that pattern and you notice straight away, but if it lies undisturbed it effectively becomes invisible or forgotten.

To do this analysis successfully, pretend you are the prospect you created a profile for earlier and look at your own business through their eyes. A kind of prospect x-ray specs approach.

Cast out the features and replace them with benefits and before you know it staff will start saying things like "I didn't know we did that," or "Is that something new we do?" (Resist the desire to cause physical injury, remember you probably pay them, not the other way around!)

Most businesses struggle at Facts Match and this is why it is the area that is characteristically the narrowest in all three business shapes: the Funnel, the Hourglass and the Terrarium.

Effort at this level will open up the bucket in both directions and the flow of consumers will start.

That said, with so much choice at hand for prospects the final decision may require one more element of the relationship build, **the test drive**.

4. Response

A quick review of your sales process will reveal your response marketing strategy. This step is primarily characterised by face-to-face engagement. This does not necessarily always involve human interaction. It is better to think of it as brand-face to prospect-face. The nature of your business may require a salesman to do this but for most it is the shop, the website, the call centre, the point of sale or the packaging.

This is the first real opportunity to have a conversation. However the conversation is not with someone you know; it is with someone who is testing you out to see if you are worth having.

These people don't care what you know; they want to know that you care.

Now is not the time to throw an incentive at them randomly. The idea of a family holiday to Disney or the chance to win a free ipod or pampering weekend might sound great but does it have anything to do with your product or service? More critically does it demonstrate one of your benefits? Will it help change or form an opinion of your value at this stage in the decision-making process? Getting prospects here has been really tough so to miss out on the chance of demonstrating a benefit at this point is again simply wasteful.

In choosing a benefit that you are going to let people experience, try and pick one that:

a **Does not cost a fortune to provide.**

In the late 90s a new Internet provider decided to target families with university-aged children with a service that would enable parents to more easily communicate to their children from a PC through to their mobile phones. They offered free internet usage for the students as an incentive. Within two years there were over 200,000 users of the service. Unfortunately all were students communicating with each other. Revenue stream – zero. The company folded the day the venture capital dried up.

b **Gives as close to the full experience as possible but with limits (in time span and scope).**
If your product or service has any form of ongoing activity or different levels then this is a good way of giving people a go. In the early days of PlayStation games it was not uncommon to cover-mount a game demo on a gamers' magazine. This approach still works well today, giving gamers a real experience of the game and inspiring purchase of the full version.

When First Telecom (one of the first least-cost routing telephone companies to emerge after the deregulation of BT's monopoly) launched their corporate package, the strategy was to analyse a phone bill and identify which one country destination received most international call traffic. By isolating this call traffic, say to India, the cost savings could be applied to the calls to this country only. Within a month, a 70% saving could be demonstrated. Almost all of the clients that signed up to this went on to switch the rest of all their calls through First Telecom.

The traditional test drive still works best.
The motor industry has the test drive built into their sales process but there is nothing to prevent any other business using this approach. This is often an expensive option but any form of "try me and if you are not happy return it within a specific time period" is a test drive.

The likes of M&S and Argos are famous for their no-quibble money-back guarantees, and catalogue retailers are happy to send you items on a "return if not happy" basis, the better ones including a return bag as part of their customer service.

Sale or return. This is the ultimate incentive to try. Works especially well for third party distribution channels because they only have to pay you when a sale is made. By taking this approach you are incentivising the route to market by de-risking the investment for the distributor. This risk however is at your door with returns a real danger to your business especially if seasonality or optimising storage are part of the distributors stock management strategy.

Cross selling. This is a common form of test drive for consumable products. Buy a shampoo, get a free conditioner. Take one recipe, try another free. This route often presents itself as buy one get one free (BOGOF) when in fact it is a try me free promotion attached to a product people are already disposed to buy. A good way to develop a purchase repertoire amongst existing customers but less likely to bring in completely new consumers.

There are many other ways of getting the benefit across to your prospect but the above tend to be the most commonly used.

Whatever you do, try and avoid the promotion trap or the discount trap.

The Promotion Trap

The promotion trap has developed to an art in its own right, with self-liquidating promotions, where the brand-owner insures against the cost of redemption by making the customer pay combining collecting coupons or pack-tops with a small cash contribution. Whilst this can up sales as people buy more, they are rarely any more sales generative in the long run. Promotional people tend to put together incentives that the buyer might like rather than anything that will leave a brand relationship legacy. A prize draw might sound great for the winner but does little for the crispy bar, cereal or shoe polish that it appears on.

It can also play havoc with your own stock control. In the early 90s, Brooke Bond ran a "collect a dinosaur" promotion on their best selling PG Tips brand. Each box of tea bags had one of six dinosaurs lovingly taped to the top. As you walked past the display, a remote device would raw like a Tyrannosaurus Rex drawing your attention to the tea.

The rate of sale went through the roof. Everyone was hugely excited until it became apparent that people were buying six packets at a time to collect the full set of dinosaurs in one go. Short-term stocking issues were met with extra deliveries.

Then stop. People had enough tea to last them six months to a year. No need to buy any more. The rate of sale plummeted to a practical standstill. Not such a great promotion after all.

Promotions are too often recommended on the basis of what has worked in the past rather than on how to match the prospect's understanding of the product or service.

The Discount Trap

Incentivising purchase through discounts has lost much of its lustre because all of us are surrounded by money-off messages to the point of madness.

Even banks have "sales". Imagine that. (You have to because such a promotion lacks any imagination at all.) Worse than that, discounting lacks any understanding of the value of the product or service being offered. If you have created a value proposition that is well presented, fair and reasonable, then discounts should make you feel uncomfortable. (In fact a clear value proposition should enable you to put your prices up!)

If ever you feel the need to incentivise sales through giving away your margin, try giving away your margin in another way.

Spend it on something that will enhance your value proposition. **Added value**. Be amazed how a free bottle opener, a cleaning cloth attached to the cleaning solution bottle, a free email address, a statement holder or equivalent can add to the perception of your product or service. It differentiates you from the competition and makes your product more appealing. A discount just means spending less. Money forgotten the moment the next purchase is made. Added value leaves a legacy that often lives well beyond the moment of purchase.

Getting people to have an unconditional trial of your product or service shouldn't be too hard to add into your marketing plan but make sure there is always activity in this area. Get this right and you will see a whole host of new users. But this new relationship you have with them was likely to have been generated under false pretences. Motivated by incentive, often these prospects do not feel entirely locked to your value proposition, so this must come next.

5. Usage

Spending time thinking about what your customers actually get for their money can be one of the most cathartic aspects of reviewing your own Brand Bucket®. The day-to-day routine of servicing your customers brings with it a massive assumption that all is well. Everything is in order. Happy staff, happy customers. The trouble is that we all become so focused on delivering the goods that the value to the customer is also assumed and rarely reviewed.

The usage step is where the real value equation comes into play:

Value = cost + received benefit

The act of running a business places focus on internal processes that are inevitably orientated towards cost management so emphasis on benefits is diluted if not lost altogether. The resulting corporate culture naturally becomes task-related.

Often by asking customers why they bought from you, this will bring to life aspects of your business that you have taken for granted or considered unimportant. A few coffee chats with your top customers will soon reveal why they value you, and often there are things that only you can offer. By reintroducing these aspects into your business they become value drivers that can be celebrated and used to attract prospects and keep customers loyal.

Implementing a "why our customers love us" campaign into your marketing plan will bring immediate results. By asking your staff this question, they will find new pride in their work. After all, they are the ones delivering the value proposition.

Often staff will add other benefits that they know people like but have never thought to say before. Customers will soon see a change of attitude which will remind them why they became customers in the first place as well as qualify why they remain as such! No relationship is ever perfect but if on the whole the balance of power is with the benefits received rather than cost, then loyalty is more likely.

Take the customer journey from beginning to end in your mind and you will soon develop a picture of what it is like to be a customer and identify the good experiences as well as the maybe not so good ones.

Strong businesses have systematically "flat-packed" this experience so there can be no doubt in the consumer's mind as to what to expect and what they will get.

6. Loyalty

If a business delivers its promise and creates reliable, consistent value for the consumer then you have at your disposal the most valuable asset a marketing plan can have.

By becoming part of the consumers' lifestyle, your brand has also become part of the way they see themselves. Part of their self image. Their reputation is now entirely aligned with yours. How they are seen by their mother, father, teacher, employee, friend, team-mate, colleague, daughter, son, boss, is entirely linked with your brand promise. They are now defined by your value proposition. Quite some responsibility whether you are a cheesy string, a life insurance or an airline!

No matter how clever your marketing plan, the most powerful marketing tool is something you have least control over: word of mouth.

Give a bad experience and no matter how much marketing money you spend, you cannot prevent word of mouth springing a leak in your Brand Bucket$^{®}$. It is said in the bar trade that if you upset one customer you lose nine others. To minimise the effect of bad experience, the first thing you should undertake is to define your "crisis management" strategy for an upset customer. How do you handle a complaint and more importantly what do you do about putting it right? Incidentally this is one of the areas good PR agencies are excellent at helping you put together.

Experience shows that the way a customer complaint is resolved can lead to long-term loyalty. Why? It is simply because the customer has invested considerable time, effort and money in building a relationship with you.

They may even have put their own reputation on the line too, so giving this up is not the preferred option. In resolving any dispute or dissatisfaction you are working the value proposition to its maximum effect and as a result re-endorsing their belief about the brand. **Through adversity the brand relationship can be strengthened.**

A well-formed problem-resolution strategy can cut down on disproportionate effort required to attain an equitable solution when things go wrong. What can go wrong will and probably all at the same time on top of the normal daily routine as well! Resolving complaints can often take longer than the sale in the first place!

Problem resolution is obviously less of an issue for businesses who understand the need to provide value – and any losses resulting are often compensated for by referrals.

Referrals are a business-owner's dream come true. Get enough of them and you can kick that marketing plan into touch.... or can you?

Referrals are everything you could hope for. An existing customer has become your new sales force and recommended you to someone you don't even know, suggesting that they should come and buy from you. What more could you ask for?

Well, without controlling the journey into The Brand Bucket® you run a big risk.

The promise this new prospect has been given was one made by a consumer, not you the brand-owner. It therefore might be misleading, incorrect or simply not true. On top of this if your acquisition journey does not reference this promise, the conversion of this prospect is going to be tougher, more expensive and more likely to go wrong.

And yet you will feel duty-bound to service this prospect in a special way because they are connected to an existing customer. If you upset the referred prospect you are potentially weakening the relationship with the existing customer and even risk breaking it altogether. The "I don't know why you recommended them to me" response punches another gaping hole in your Brand Bucket®.

These "organic referrals" should have their own special Brand Bucket® journey on your marketing plan.

Better still is to put in an extra line on your marketing plan which incentivises referrals. Call them your advocate referral programme.

The advocate referral programme

This marketing tool can be invaluable to your business in a number of ways.

It is a great excuse to have a conversation with your existing customers. It can only be a feel-good piece of communication because you are going to ask people to refer your brand through one of the perceived benefits.

This is a great opportunity to remind your existing customers why they are using you or even introduce them to a benefit they have forgotten or haven't used themselves. Plus you can incentivise them to recommend your brand to someone they know.

But there is a rule that must be obeyed at this point:

Whatever incentive you offer, **exactly the same value must be offered to both the referred and referee.**

Anything else is corporate bribery.

For example you allocate a budget of £40 as an incentive:

		Risk:	Outcome:
Option 1	Recommend a friend and receive £40 shopping vouchers.	Your friend finds out you got paid to recommend them.	Friendship under stress. A corporate bribe.
Option 2	Recommend a friend and they get £40 off their purchase.	Customer feels used. Nothing in it for them.	Existing relationship stressed. A corporate bribe.
Option 3	Recommend a friend and get a bottle of champagne (worth £20) and they get a bottle of champagne (worth £20).	None – both parties feel good about the brand.	Two happy customers with a thank you from the brand.

When auditing your referral marketing, review your incentive schemes against the above.

Get talking

The final part of loyalty marketing is how often you converse with your customers. Most businesses that offer any kind of service should have in place a loyalty scheme on their marketing plan.

In the past these were put together by promotional agencies who were more interested in finding an outlet for affinity products or services (that includes products and services from their friends!) and/or cheap goods from China with a good margin on them. Once again this serviced the wrong recipient of loyalty.

A new set of screwdrivers or a wind-up torch seems on the face of it quite handy but when the consumer works out they have to spend £800 getting them and the fact that previous experience suggests they will probably break on first use, then the appeal wears off. Rest assured the promotions agency has taken *its* profits, though.

The key to successful loyalty schemes is that they should promise access to even more value from your brand. Carefully managed, this can enable you to introduce new products and services or add value to existing products and service.

Just making people feel good about you with an unrelated gift will have only short-term effect and will push your brand quickly into the second-hand market.

Try and ringfence the promotions too. Currently one airline has so many air miles in circulation that if everyone cashed them in, they would have to run the company with no revenue for up to 2 years. Unlikely to occur but it is still something that needs to be insured against. Identify those loyalty schemes which lead to your brand benefits. Discard all others.

There are other loyalty mechanics: newsletters/magazines;

email blasts; blogs; and community websites. The trouble with these is that they are expensive to maintain well, targeted generically, and so are more at the broadcast top of The Brand Bucket® than the conversational bottom of The Brand Bucket®.

Plus in a world of information overload all these are probably only welcomed by the most loyal anyway. In a digital world where daily newspapers are out of date as they leave the presses, receiving a monthly or quarterly newsletter is hardly going to set the world alight.

If, however, they are aligned with changes in legislation or even consumer behaviour, or give topical advice tips or tricks, then they can really add value.

Look after your consumers as if they were customers with potential (to buy more) and make them feel valued, and they will reward you with more business.

It is now time to audit your business and review your business at each level of The Brand Bucket®. Using the chart below, rate how you feel you are performing at each of the 6 steps through The Brand Bucket®. **Rate each of these Strong, Medium or Weak.**

In a matter of moments you will have created a good snapshot of the shape your brand marketing is in and where emphasis can be placed to drive more prospects through your Brand Bucket®:

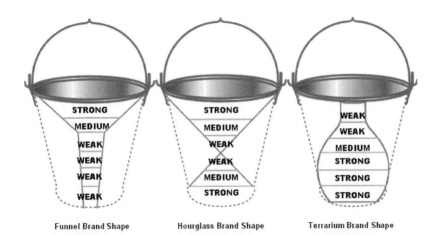

Funnel Brand Shape   Hourglass Brand Shape   Terrarium Brand Shape

8

TURNING YOUR MARKETING SHAPE INTO A BRAND BUCKET® SHAPE

What to do if you have a funnel shape

This is one of the more difficult shapes for a business and can cause the most angst at board level.

"We've spent all this money raising awareness of the brand, and yet nobody is buying."

Now of course it may well be there is a problem with prices, product or availability, but one hopes these were considered before the marketing campaign was signed off. If not, these need to be adjusted accordingly. Make sure anything you adjust, however, remains true to the value proposition. Slashing prices without deference to the value proposition can damage the brand beyond repair.

All too often the problem lies with the nature of the marketing effort. If broadcast media are in use, then the chances are enough people will know who you are. The Brand Bucket® tells us this is not enough but before we put in place remedial marketing activity, we need to understand what being "well known" actually means.

Case study: Heineken

Heineken for many years used the line: "Heineken refreshes the parts other beers cannot reach."

In the early nineties a clever agency persuaded the client that this was so ingrained in people's minds that rather than trot out another demonstration of this idea they could move it on with an end line: "Only Heineken can do this."

After years of refreshing the parts, within 18 months, research amongst lager drinkers found them asking the question: only Heineken can do *what*?

They have never really recovered.

The best way to understand how "well known" you really are is to ask a few people **what** they know about you. Be prepared to find out that it is probably very little. If there has been a "creative" spin to your advertising then they may recall that; they might replay your jingle or ditty. They may even have some vague idea of what you do based on your name, but beyond that there is likely to be little or no sense of where you fit into their lives or why they might need your brand.

The fix is relatively simple. Seek out every benefit you can lay your hands on and add them into your communication at every level of the marketing mix. Your whole marketing effort needs to act like a directory of how you are going to improve everyone's lives when using your product. Because they have heard of you, very quickly people will either see your brand as a viable alternative to something they are using already or as a great new addition to their brand portfolio. Aim for "now I know why I like you".

Replace the so-called brand awareness-building campaigns with branded benefit-led ads. Imagine you are trying to steal customers from your competitors (they are probably doing it to you at this very moment) and demonstrate how you are more impressive on the benefits front.

Now turn your attention to your response campaigns and delight your prospects. Let your prospects try you out.

By turning your whole marketing mix towards benefits, very soon the prospect who claimed to know you will pour further down into The Brand Bucket$^®$ and towards the purchase point.

The money invested at the top of the bucket is now being utilised and converted to cash sales. In fact, some regard this as the "purchase tipping point", the point at which a prospect converts into a customer. By directly involving your prospect in your benefit story, they will see proof that you will deliver what you promise to deliver. This proof is the key to changing the funnel into a bucket.

Make your response campaign relevant to your benefits list **not** to your image. We'd all love to win something for nothing but at this time you need to be entirely focused on sales. Your prospect has already passed through the image dimension, and spending more money on simply getting them to feel good about you does not bring them closer to the purchase tipping point. (Don't be distracted by the promise of creating a database of people who enter your winner-takes-all competition. What would you do with them then? Of course, tell them about your features and benefits. No wait a minute... they've gone elsewhere!)

> **KEY ACTION:** Pick a key aspect of your brand promise that translates into a must have benefit and build a "take a test drive" story around that one benefit.

You'll see long-term results to your bottom line. And DO NOT allow your image dimensions to drive the process; they should be referenced not enhanced. This is the wrong time to do it.

Think Hoover/Free flights to New York and ask *why* (we all know the "what"!).

Think cross channel Ferries and £1 trips to France and ask *why* – a full experience at a fraction of the cost, now that's a test drive.

So you have an hourglass brand shape, what next?

With an hourglass shape the chances are that, as a business-owner, you are totally confused. You are generating sales, getting referrals even, and when you go out into the marketplace people seem to have heard of you. And yet sales are static or even in decline. Again, if there are no other obvious flaws in the product or price, then marketing can be the problem or solution.

Your design agency keeps coming up with irresistible new ideas for "building your brand" and pouring more people into the top of your bucket and yet sales are not shifting. There is clearly a break in the sales process.

There are two possible causes for this:

1. Your loyalists are not buying the brand for the reasons you think they are.
2. The perception of your brand amongst prospects does not link to the value proposition.

To fix this, you need to understand how the prospect **and** the consumer feel about your brand.

Research amongst existing customers and prospects who are aware of you will give you these insights.

This might throw up a mismatch which when remedied will restart the flow of prospects through The Brand Bucket®.

The standard way to do this is to change perceptions at the top of the bucket. Often called rebranding by the marketing industry, this is rarely the full answer.

How often do brands "reposition" or re-brand only for brand-owners to realise that, after what often constitutes significant investment, opinions of existing consumers have either not changed or have become confused, and those who were yet to buy have still not bought.

The need for change in the marketing effort is not just at the top of the bucket; it quite distinctly requires renewed effort in the middle too. By talking to existing consumers you should aim to unearth the benefits that they value and push these up through the bucket towards the prospect.

Because awareness and image already have some pre-programmed dimensions in place, even with a totally new approach to the top via a rebrand, you can only change the perceptions through client experience. Simply telling them you've changed will not be enough; you have to evoke a change in behaviour. In this way you can reinstall your brand at image level in a newer and, because it is experientially derived, more relevant way. By doing this, the thinnest part of your "hourglass" will widen, releasing those at the top of the bucket and driving them towards the bottom.

Use product placement, affinity marketing, sponsorship, packaging changes, point of sale, benefit-led promotions and even live brand experiences to widen the middle of your hourglass.

More importantly, if you insist on using broadcast media, use it to explain the change rather than simply announce the change.

So you have a terrarium brand shape, what next?

This shape creeps up on you and suddenly your business is in trouble. It is the one most business-owners feel comfortable with and yet is the most dangerous of all three shapes.

Surrounded by lots of loyal customers being serviced by loyal staff, every trip out into "consumerland" is greeted by reassuring noises that all is well with the world.

Suddenly you're de-listed, your biggest client gets taken over and changes supplier, 5% of your customers simply disappear through death and move-aways, a competitor launches a better, faster, cheaper product.

You adopt protectionist strategies, reduce your prices, renew your contacts and look for new markets. At its worst, you install blame culture. But eventually you run out of fingers to plug the holes in the bucket (or dyke) and you seek out outside help to market your product.

The trouble is that this takes time, which is running out, and money, which (if you had any) is also disappearing fast. Unfortunately simply opening the top of the bucket is not the fastest or cheapest solution.

> **KEY ACTION: Decide what the main threat is to the business.**

A brief competitive review will guide you towards one of two possible market strategies: Brand Steal or Market Growth.

1. Brand Steal

If it's possible to present the benefits of the product or service in a way that beats the competition, then this strategy should be adopted.

This is not to say you should knock your competition. But you should.

There has never been a better time to demonstrate to the competition how your product or service can benefit people more. You have permission to be brave because in your heart you know your customers like your value proposition.

Demonstrate your superiority at every level of The Brand Bucket®, in your ads (watch the industry rules), on your website, at the exhibitions, in the brochures, in your customer letters, on your invoices. Leave no marketing stone unturned.

For the good of your business steal share from the others. Of course, if you don't have any benefits over and above the competition or you are selling a unique service then market growth is the other way.

2. Market Growth

If it is apparent that the benefits are matched or exceeded by the competition or, as is more likely, the market is saturated, then the marketing should be focused on opening up new markets.

Back to the psychographic profiling and your value proposition and go and look for new groups of people who, with a slightly different strategy for engagement, might be attracted to your products or services for the first time. If Tesco can sell pet insurance and mortgages there's hope for everyone.

For terrarium businesses and with either or both strategies above to hand, the most important task is to segment your customer asset base.

This is the mainstay of the terrarium business and it is helpful to categorise customers into different groups:

1. Those most likely to leak from your bucket
2. Those that need additional ongoing care
3. Those who will willingly act as brand ambassadors
4. Those to whom you should do nothing more but nothing less.

Managing Group 1

The first group require almost immediate remedial action as they are most likely to "churn" and are often called "switchers", attracted to the best offer in town. They are likely to using your brand at a very rational level and are actively watching the competitive set ,so will be easily tempted away by the perception of better benefits from another brand. The key here is *perception*. Rarely is the grass greener but because they are not sufficiently emotionally engaged, they are more easily tempted away.

This group need to learn to enjoy being a customer of yours again. They need to feel valued, part of your brand club.

By implementing a "thank you" communications strategy you can reengage these customers easily. You can offer free (but relevant) gifts, a tips letter (cf a newsletter that is actually useful), additional benefits, additional brand synergies with other products. There are many ways to do this. Remember the result you want from such a campaign is "thank you" or "that's good". Do not try and sell them something. This will send them scattering to your competitors straight away.

You are simply looking to strengthen the emotional ties with your brand.

In this way your competitors must start at the top of their own buckets and this is clearly more challenging than simply stealing your customer.

Managing Group 2

The second group differ from the first only in that they are less likely to be actively looking around for alternatives. That said, if you ignore them, they might be tempted away with no notice at all. This group need very gentle reminders that you value them. Some additional product information, tips for them to get more from using your products, opportunities to try new things.

The communication hierarchy should be dominated by a "we value you" message. Be careful to demonstrate that you are genuinely interested in them, not just pretending to "care". For example in this e-card world, a printed Christmas card can be nice but printing signatures on the inside is not as strong as one person signing personally with a short message. The same goes for birthday cards. Try and be unexpected. This will leave a longer legacy than anything else for this group. Simple acknowledgement is all it takes.

Managing Group 3

The third group are very special. Not only are they happy to continue to use your brand, they see it as a contributor to defining who they are and where they see themselves in the world.

So much so that they will willingly tell other people about how you make a difference to their lives.

This group of people are your strongest brand ambassadors. They are probably acting as advocates of your brand whenever they get a chance. And here is the opportunity to grow your business cheaply and quickly. Take the chance and randomness out of this advocacy.

As it is, should your brand become relevant in a conversation, then you may well be mentioned. It is likely that this will occur naturally in the pub, over lunch, outside the school gates, over dinner, before a meeting, in the canteen, on the bus home, etc. Hardly the place to do a product demonstration or present a service. More importantly you have no control over when this conversation emerges, how it is dealt with and how long the message lasts with the prospects.

Remember every day we are bombarded with over 4,000 new marketing messages, so your message is likely to get diluted very quickly until it is probably discarded. Being remembered is all a matter of chance when it comes to surviving these odds.

In the immediate term you should **incentivise these brand ambassadors** to recommend a friend. This will act as a shortcut through the top of the bucket and bring in new prospects straight into the Facts Match level in the bucket because the referrer has added their own image dimensions to your sales process.

The corresponding incentive should be aligned with a brand steal or market growth strategy and the reward equal for both the referrer and the person referred (referee).

With these in place, full-scale awareness and image campaigns should be implemented to act as a support to the customers acting as your sales agents. Do ensure this is only with the bottom up bucket metrics in mind. If you need every household in the UK then go national. If you don't need that many, behave like a national brand but in local areas or segmented by prospect type.

Rushing into a broadcast media campaign will simply create an hourglass brand shape and this will not address the fundamentals of the business need.

Managing Group 4

The fourth group are content. They do not want to be sold to; they do not want to sell for you. You are embedded in their Image Match dimensions and they need only watching. It is worth keeping them up to date with snippets of news that demonstrate you are still there to be relied on, providing reassurance they need.

Apart from that leave them alone.

For the active marketer this is hard. Surely they would want to know about features, improved benefits, similar products and services. They don't and they will only thank you for telling them by moving their business elsewhere. So it is imperative that you know who these people are. Unfortunately they are hardest to find because they don't want you to find them.

If you do find them, then you can treat them to a little thank-you every now and then, a special event for your favourite, trouble-free customers. But don't try and sell to them. They'll react badly.

9

PUTTING TOGETHER YOUR ONE-PAGE MARKETING PLAN

All too often organisations run their marketing without a plan. Like any journey, having no map to guide you is a very quick way of getting lost.

If you have a good idea of what shape your business is in, then putting together a one-page marketing plan is the best way to ensure your bucket is working.

It is said that if you fail to plan, you plan to fail, but planning for planning's sake is just as dangerous.

Many businesses toil over plans that take weeks to conceive, craft and agree, including a complete audit of previous results, forecasts and research.

Remember, if you take longer than three weeks someone somewhere (probably in China) has copied your product, improved on it, tooled its manufacture, made and shipped enough stock to blow a hole in your plan. For service businesses, India offers much the same.

That doesn't mean making the common mistake of:

"Let's just do what we know. No need to plan."

If you recognise these comments then you are more likely to become one of the four out of five businesses that fail in the long run.

There are two types of plans. Directional one-page plans and more detailed investor plans. You may need both, but you definitely need one. A marketing plan, like a business plan, needs only one page. A tiller of the yacht. A helicopter view of your business and how it works.

Call it what you will, but a one-page marketing plan should compliment your business plan. It is no good for the investors but it will help the brand-owner steer the business in the right direction.

It should be visionary, ambitious and have measurable results within it.

An implementation plan need only be short-term.

Twelve months is a good starting point although seasonal, quarterly or "by product availability" make good one-page marketing plans too. This plan is detailed. It should show, what, where, when, how much and what are the expected effects. This plan represents the instructions for the crew, what they should do and what is expected of them.

It provides a regular viewpoint to check and adjust. Just as the wind changes so does consumer behaviour, and you need to be able to adjust.

Looking at this plan should make you perspire a little. It should require effort, it should contain a mix of things you know work and a couple of things that should work and a few things that if they worked would change everything.

The one-page plan is a working tool. It is something that everyone involved in communication with prospects and customers should be aware of, and identifies what their role is in delivering the plan.

The following illustration represents the typical elements that might be considered in a one-page marketing plan:

MEASURE, MEASURE, MEASURE

	THE DESIRED METRICS	COMMUNICATION OBJECTIVES	KEY COMPONENTS OF ACTION PLAN
AWARENESS	Number of people required to reach. Conversion ratio 10:1	- Name registration - Logo recognition	Raise awareness only to level of reach required. Consider measurable broadcast media: advertising; networking; exhibitions; Google/Yahoo; direct mail; leaflet drops; email blasts; public speaking.
IMAGE MATCH	Number of information packs, visits to website, calls to call centre etc to get test drives. Start with ratio 10:1	- Consistent brand look and feel - Benefit led tagline - "For me" imagery	
FACTS MATCH	Number of test drives, trials, audits required to get sales. This is a conversion ratio (3-5:1)	Benefits, benefits, benefits	Review brochure; website; sales presentations on pack text; point of sale; directory listings and copy.
RESPONSE		A no commitment trial of the benefits (with commercial limits)	Create test drive programmes: seminars; audits; quotes; free trials; money back guarantees; sale or return
USAGE	Number of sales. WHAT, HOW MUCH AND WHEN	We do what we say we do at every point of interaction	Review call centre scripts; revisit customer service dept; review on pack copy; user guides. Put benefits at heart of brand use.
LOYALTY		Look after customers. Incentivise referrals. Defined complaints procedure.	Review regular contact strategy. Create incentivised recommend a friend scheme. Ensure organic referrals are treated differently. Install customer complaints procedure.

THE PROSPECT

A brief description of The psychographic Profile of your ideal Prospect goes here

10

CREATING A BRAND PROPERTY

With a one-page plan in place and your brand audit completed, it is now time to make sure that the whole prospect journey is integrated and unified as one.

Where does the call-centre operation fit in? How does the website integrate into the brand story? What about the brochures, the ads, the reception, the staff training, the warehouse, the products? What do customer letters say, how do leads get followed up, what the salesmen are using, how do they dress, what is your recruitment policy? All of these things and hundreds more affect the propensity to buy the product or service.

Each has a role in generating a sale; each element should link to every other one. By doing this, then every time a customer interacts with your brand, no matter how small this interaction, they should know that it is your brand that they are involved with. This is the foundation of a shatterproof brand.

Take for example the Coca-Cola bottle. The design brief for this was to create a glass shape that when smashed ensured that each broken piece was still clearly recognisable as coming from a coke bottle. The brief was met and today that iconic shape remains at the heart of the brand (even if it is plastic now!) Take the Rolls Royce radiator, beautifully crafted to the point where that shape is a highly protected trademark – or the 57 on the side of a Heinz Ketchup, an iconic application that when interrogated has almost no meaning and yet is key to the relationship with that brand today.

> The Heinz '57' often associated with varieties was entirely made up. Mr Heinz was riding on an elevated train when he spotted a poster advertising 125 pairs of shoes. Taken by the use of a number he settled on the number 57 and proceeded to own the number with large illuminated billboards, changing their telephone and address numbers to include the number 57, and generally sponsoring anything to do with 57. Now the number is synonymous with Heinz products.

Making your brand shatterproof is key to ensuring that when you spend money on building a relationship with your customer, it all adds to the value that people place on your brand. No matter what point of interaction you look at in your business – the brand touchpoints – the same shatterproof approach should be obvious.

At your disposal are three core communication areas to do this:

1. The look and feel
2. The messaging
3. The product itself

To make your brand shatterproof, you must have **at least two** of these operating at the same time. If there is only one, then the brand will be much more susceptible to competitors, and when you have all three operating together the relationship will be strengthened each time your customer interacts with the product or service.

In auditing your brand touchpoints you need to identify and evaluate the strength of each against the three areas. For example:

- Do your customer letters look and feel as if they come from the product or simply from a computer?

- Does the title on the front of your brochure come from the brand story?

- Does the design of your reception area reflect the business you are in?

- Can you see the packaging in your advertising – can you see your advertising in your packaging?

Consider everything, the cups in the canteen, the uniforms of the security staff, the signs in the car park, the noticeboard, the email sign-off, your franking machine, your business cards, your meeting room pads, and so on.

Each and every touchpoint must be audited.

1. Look and feel

Everything must reflect the essence of the brand.

Good design can do this, and placing a strong hint of it on every brand touchpoint brings everything together. A picture says a thousand words. A good design property can often do the same. It acts to remind, it acts to endorse. It acts as a signpost to let the customer know where they are at all times.

Think how reassured you feel when, after driving a long distance, eventually the signpost for your destination appears at the side of the road and guides you to your eventual destination. Look and feel has exactly the same impact on the decision-making process and helps you resist competitor distraction.

2. Messaging

In defining your brand story in the form of a Brand Galvaniser™, you have a very flexible tool for your messaging. Any construction of messages from this will service the central differentiating core.

Every brand touchpoint must reference your value proposition. Each piece of communication becomes a voice, all conveying the same value story time and time again. In this way your story becomes embedded in the mind of your consumer. The more embedded it becomes, the harder it becomes for competitors to knock your product out of the way.

By using all the messages on the Brand Galvaniser™ whenever you can, this ensures that the story has many dimensions to it. This is critical to the long-term relationship. If you rely solely on one message, then others can come in a do that message better and you will lose out.

3. The product

Clearly, given that the brand emerges directly from the product or service, this should be the easiest bit, but too often organisations become complacent about their own products and services. They take the good bits for granted. It is human nature to do this.

Do you have pictures hanging on your wall at home? Do you admire them every day? I doubt it. Not because you don't like them (you did when you put them up originally). It is simply that your mind has logged them and they form part of the daily pattern to which you have become accustomed. If someone moves a picture, you'll notice it straight away! Working in an organisation is no different. Very quickly people effectively "forget" the product they work with.

It is imperative that you actively remind yourself of what makes your product fantastic. Every day, at every opportunity.

To do this you need to actively celebrate the things that make the product or service tick, and most important of all, record this in a way that is then seen by everyone every day. That does not mean a mission statement on the wall of the meeting room. It means making your internal communication reflect your key product differentiators. Eventually everyone will start to behave like the promise. It becomes a "mindset uniform" rather than a physical one.

Provide feedback mechanisms – a forum, workshops – and celebrate behaviour that you want everyone to replicate. Involve everyone. For example, often the person on reception has the best perception of what is going on as far as customer service is concerned.

Identify the things about your product and service that make you proud, that make you smile, that make you come to work. **Capture these and your customers will want them too.** If you merge these things with your messages and then create a look and feel that remind people of these product benefits every time you come into contact with the business, you will have created the basis of a strong relationship and a strong brand.

By now you should have at your disposal a long list of elements that define your brand. Rarely, however, do they all fit snugly together and appear connected, in a way that customers would recognise as coming from the same place.

If you take each item on the brand audit list and try and rewrite it so that it reads as a benefit of the feature you will suddenly see a very powerful story emerge. A story that as you read it makes you want it more, and the more you want it the more you read the list, challenging it to deliver the promise that is now clearly being depicted. Now you have the makings of a brand that people will value.

The emphasis must be on engaging the customer directly.

11

MATCHING THE MEDIUM TO THE MESSAGE

Over the last decade we have seen an explosion of media choice driven by the capabilities of the digital arena. And we haven't even scratched the surface of where this is all going. The result is that there are more media than ever before and their behaviour has consequently changed.

In years gone by broadcast media ruled. TV, posters and press were the main ways, if not the only ways, to reach a mass of people effectively. As a result, brands could spread news about their product quickly and with immediate results at the till. Today very few people rely on this as a definitive source of information. Sure it can heighten awareness and in some cases fulfil image dimensions, but rarely will a sale result if used in isolation.

This reliance on so-called "above the line"[3] advertising is both outdated and increasingly irrelevant.

Today we all multisource our information, combining a whole host of different sources to guide us through The Brand Bucket® process. Whether it is the internet, or Sky Sports, or Cycle News, or a leaflet, or live brand experience, or a price ad in the newspaper, or a radio programme, a podcast, an email, or what influences most of all, a recommendation from a friend or colleague, we now use the media around us to influence our

---

[3] See Appendix for definition

decisions.

It is important that you apply The Brand Bucket® to your media choice because no longer is the medium the message as was true in the past. It is no longer the case that an editor or journalist can hold court on opinion because they have diligently investigated or researched their facts. Previously we accepted the journalists' representation as fact, ignoring the personal (or professional) bias of the writer. Today the speed of communication across the globe means that opinion is short-lived, and tested almost instantaneously.

Any news that requires process (e.g. print) is out of date the moment is published, and mindful of this we are less reliant on formal communication and much more reliant on the best friend of the marketer – word of mouth.

Therefore the media that will work best for your marketing are those that either drive word of mouth or contribute word of mouth or enable word of mouth. The effectiveness of a medium is now dictated by how close a conversation you can have with your prospects and consumer. The further away, the weaker the conversation, the more waste. It is a media whirlpool and the nearer to direct peer-to-peer contact, the more likely the medium is to being successful for your brand.

With this in mind, the process of planning your media choice must start with an understanding of the consumer issue and what stage of the decision-making process they are at before you can evaluate which medium will be most effective for driving people towards purchase.

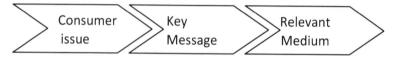

A key benefit of The Brand Bucket® is the ability to use it as a way to evaluate the relevant medium for the message. Due to media fragmentation, this is more critical than ever and supports media-owners who believe that the medium is the message. Sure if you're into history, you might watch the history channel, if you're into sport you are likely to watch the sports channels, if you are into cycling then a bike magazine will be of interest, if you like cooking then you are more likely to buy a cooking magazine.

What is no longer clear is that using these media as broadcast media has any effect on the purchase cycle or even an effect on the propensity to buy.

Not enough work is being done to really understand how consumers are thinking at the time they consume these media.

Many purchase decisions are taking place in one-to-one conversations via the internet, email, blogging (web-logging) and texting. It is here that real conversations are taking place, drawing on direct experiences.

This is not new thinking. It has always been that way. Instead of engaging millions of people with a 30-second ad in the middle of Coronation Street in the knowledge 22 million of us would see it, now we have to talk exclusively to the key influencers in society.

This is where the Brand Bucket$^{®}$ analysis can really help. By identifying the key consumer issues at each of the 6 steps and defining the creative message at each step we have created a mini-brief for the relevant media.

We can interrogate each medium in a way that is focused on delivery of the message, and map out how this medium dovetails into the behavioural mindset of our chosen prospect.

Awareness Generators:
Anything that can only deliver awareness. From blimps to branded pens, posters and taxi sides, stress balls and mints,

baseball caps and perimeter ads are all likely to be hard to justify on a marketing plan. The use of these has no conversational value at all, is easily subsumed by the other 3999 messages that day and has limited sales effect today. A shame, they once brought colour to our lives but have long been replaced by the moving image. If, however, you wish to add scale or a tail to other activity then sticking a line and logo in front of people "might" work.

Image Generators

If more than one sense is involved in a medium but the medium is passively received then these can be good for enabling people to say "I like you". TV, radio, press, cinema, Public Relations and even Sponsorship fall into this category because they can all offer sound and vision with limited interactivity. The very nature of these media is that they are expensive, with cost structures based on demographic-led thinking. It's all in the numbers. The difficulty is getting the coverage right because there is so much choice and the target market so fluid. If you want broad-scale, rapid and positive association to your brand, then these media can be powerful. For the majority of modern brands, however, they are considered less and less as part of the marketing mix.

Facts Match Generators

This is a key moment in the decision-making process – the depiction of benefits. Media that can deliver this are currently well placed to capitalise on the shift to psychographically led marketing.

The search engines are the dominant medium here, especially Google's Pay-per-click model. Whilst turning clicks into sales is reliant on ensuring the website continues the journey, the clever use of capturing the way people are thinking and immersing them in an interactive conversation immediately puts your brand ahead of the others.

Exhibitions should fall into this category, and used well, this medium can generate benefit-led desire to test out your value proposition.

The media that fall into this category need some level of commitment from the prospect: logging on, going to a venue, going shopping.

The thing to watch out for when using these media is to establish who the real target audience is and filter out the time wasters.

Response Generators

Ah the land of the promotion, free holidays and all that. These invariably waste millions of pounds for brand-owners.

The car test drive is one of the best examples of marketing at this level, but offering audits, free trials and other ways of actually experiencing at least one of your benefits provides the best media for your try-me-out message.

Usage Media

Now this area of The Brand Bucket® is rarely considered to be media-led and yet if you consider, your receipt, the packaging, the user guide, the welcome email, the courtesy call, the quote folder, the business card, the login screen – all of these are media by which you can convey your value proposition.

Loyalty Media

With your customers now firmly in your bucket, these media are some of the most important because they might just inspire repeat purchase or even recommendation. Newsletters, Tips and Tricks, loyalty points and cards, anniversary gifts, special offers – these are all media by which you can generate a stronger relationship with your brand.

Many brands have already acknowledged this and we see marketing funds being directed away from the broadcast arena and towards more direct relationship-building activity.

Today your newspaper is much more likely to be full of product-listing ads than clever ideas. With some obvious exceptions, the big brand campaigns have all but disappeared from our TV screens to be replaced by claims insurance and sale ads. This is not simply a reflection of a tougher marketplace but more because over recent years brands have seen less effective results from the old strategies of the 1990s.

If interactivity is the order of the day, then this leaves the advertising industry with little space to move in. The answer for the broadcasters has been to seek other revenue streams through things like "call to vote" celebrity-led programmes.

Where does this leave brands?

They must now look for other ways to broadcast to key influencing groups and seek out as many social influencers within that group.

They must look for places where people are actively looking for information and are willing recipients – such as shopping centres, internet search engines, blogs, etc. With so many media, with so many ways of getting messages out, with so much choice, we are now seeing media emerge that are able to build on the most powerful marketing tool humans have ever had at their disposal – word of mouth.

Advocacy, recommendation, referral, endorsement, experience, interactivity – all of these are descriptors that you should recognise when marketing your business through a chosen media.

Anything that cannot deliver these is almost guaranteed not to provide any return on investment.

That said, if a medium does not deliver against the above it does not necessarily mean it has no role. What it means is that it **must** link directly to another medium that does.

Let us look at a few of the common media and using The Brand Bucket® see what they can deliver.

Using the best media can offer

This section is simply an introduction to the common types of media that you can use to generate interest in your business.

It's written as a guide to prevent you getting sucked in by highly crafted media-owner pitches most of whom have only one sales process in mind and it isn't yours! Imagine your bucket is full of water and in the centre is a whirlpool. The flaw: by committing this section to print, I will immediately date the thinking – however, I hope that it will provide a useful snapshot of the options presently available at the time of going to press.

Public Relations (PR)

There's no easy place to start with the media whirlpool, so public relations is as good a place as any, not least because its effectiveness is currently the subject of hotly contested debate.

Some PR specialists suggest that PR is worth more than three times the value of advertising because the message comes with the endorsement of the media-owner. Now whilst there are many highly respected media out there, all potential consumers know that there is always more than one choice. A balanced piece of public relations would recognise this but often there is no such evaluation in the published piece – and where there is, the viewpoint is purely that of the writer and is often based on using product that they have been given free.

The question for PR for your business is: does it bring people into your Brand Bucket® in a way that qualifies the prospect?

PR has many excellent outcomes – crisis management strategies, lobbying, shareholder news and even CV-enhancing articles for business leaders – but its role in generating sales by making your marketing work remains a matter for debate.

Television

Many were drawn to the advertising industry by the wonder of television ads. Indeed the allure of producing 30 seconds of film still remains. But it comes at a price, a price that certainly few clients can now afford. TV has become pure luxury. In the 80s TV was used to advertise the new Ford Sierra. Perhaps not the most spectacular car in the world but after one 60-second spot in the central break of *News at 10,* the following day the showrooms were full of fleet buyers and interested prospects.

Effective because there were only four TV channels on your TV (indeed only five programmable switches too!) – and only two with a mass audience. The result: 12 million decision-makers watched News at 10 *and* the commercial break in the middle.

Can you imagine that happening today?

TV has lost its captive audience. Now there are literally hundreds of channels (according of Ofcom there were 480 channels available to UK audiences in Q2 2009), and viewers happily flick between channels with their remotes or use recording devices to skip the ads.

No longer do we rely on TV to find out about new products.

We rarely see our regular household items represented in a 30-second commercial as the likes of Unilever and Proctor and Gamble have taken much of their advertising agendas elsewhere. Those that are left are of course blessed with big marketing budgets and have been convinced by the men in the ivory towers that it is still the fastest way to get to the most people. The trouble is that TV only delivers Awareness and Image Match. Consumers no longer use the TV break as a source of information. The only businesses that can afford to use TV are those where the consumer pays the price for the medium through high margin in the product like cars, insurance, perfume, bank loans, corporate communication (for investors), and so on.

Posters – 48-Sheet and 96-Sheet Supersites

If you want to give your brand scale, one of the best ways is with large roadside posters. They say that on average, a driver on a regular journey will see your poster 38 times. Good for awareness, but for action, slightly harder. As a 3-second medium (the time it takes to go past the poster), it is often hard to write down the web address or telephone number or indeed read any more than six words. And even if you have a photographic memory or even a mobile phone to hand, the very act of continuing to drive safely will inevitably erode the memorability of the message.

Where posters can be used to best effect is not at Awareness/Image Match level but at Usage as part of an ongoing user experience providing information (i.e. carwash 150 yards on the left; new superstore opening 28th March; Sale now on, etc.)

Well branded information posters can really help in local areas.

Another great use is the special builds, ones with 3D or something unique about them. Whilst only the people who drive past them will see them, they do provide a fantastic opportunity for additional publicity and can add value to your campaign well beyond the reach of the site itself. Not cheap though!

Generally, posters disappear off the media schedule quickly as they are an expensive medium to use really well and measuring the results is hard. Not only that, the lead times are long with ten days to put them up, and ten days to print them on average.

Smaller posters – bus sides/stations/shopping centres/ street furniture

So, given the limitations of the bigger poster sites, there is an equivalent set for people on foot. You see them almost everywhere now with the digital ones even moving.

Write down the last five you have seen. If you remember any, it won't be five. And here lies the rule.

In the 70s there was an unbranded campaign featuring a young girl supported by the line "My name is Amy and I like slugs and snails", run by the poster company Adshel, to prove the effectiveness of the smaller poster medium. It created all sorts of publicity and led to many more bus-stop posters sites being installed. But no-one factored in 110% penetration of mobile phones, plasma screens in shop windows, iPods and millions more people who you need to avoid bumping into.

Set this against a backdrop that no-one has found us any more time in the day to do even more things, the net outcome is that these posters suffer in the same way as roadside posters. When do any of us stop to absorb them long enough to take in the full message? Again, they can be really effective in advertising offers outside stores, but with shelf-management timelines being so much shorter you need to plan your poster campaign very carefully if you are going to use it at Usage level as point of sale.

Cinema

Cinema has enjoyed resurgence in recent times with an increase of 6% year on year in 2009. With over 60% of visitors between the ages of 6 and 34, this is a great way of capturing a younger audience into the top of your bucket.

The appeal of cinema is born out of high-end computer-led effects that even on a big screen at home are hard to replicate, and need to be viewed on the biggest screen with the best sound system.

Now here is the challenge for the advertiser and brand-owner. Can you match the expectation of the audience who have paid to be there (an average of £5.18 per seat in 2009) at a time when the popcorn and fizzy drinks are of more interest?

It's a big ask and for most brand-owners this powerful Image Match medium is beyond them. Shame, those young ones are damn hard to track down normally!

National Press

In 1990 the circulation of the *Sun* was regularly over 4 million with possibly over 10 million readers. There were just over 3 million in March 2010 with a readership of 7.7 million.

The population of the UK has risen to 62 million in that time with much of the growth being in *Sun* readership territory. Notwithstanding this, the *Sun* has seen a significant drop in its circulation, as have all the available newspapers over the last decade.

On the 30th March 1996, the Sun sold its highest ever number of full price papers, a total of 4,783,359

We have all become time-poor, surviving in a modern day working with digital everything supposedly making our lives easier. It means we have become a "soundbite" culture where snapshot decisions are made based on snapshot information. A newspaper is considered. You need to block out the world, read and absorb. And the world won't let you.

For advertisers this is a disaster because even amongst readers, the chance of your ad actually being read let alone leading to any lasting behavioural change is so small now that press advertising is almost totally ineffective.

Again, as part of a wide-scale multimedia campaign or if you have a strong promotional "today only" message, it can work. There are nevertheless still some successful titles. In London a paper called *Metro* was launched and follows an editorial style that behaves like a news scrapbook. Literally hundreds of snippets of thought-provoking features and short articles that act as a barometer of the thinkers of the day. A bus queue chat without a bus stop. Easy to consume, something for everyone.

Swedish medium launched in 1995 now in 18 countries with 56 editions

Launched by Associated Newspapers in 1999 in London – now in 14 urban centres in UK

In only a few years that formula is working in over 14 urban centres in the UK. The business model is based on advertising revenues only so it can be expensive to advertise in.

The success of *Metro* shows that broadcast media still has a role but because of the expense you need to focus very much on the psychographic profile (described earlier).

Your ads must be consistent with the environment in which they appear and map closely to the Image Match dimensions in your bucket. You need to match to the prospect's frame of mind exactly at the time of reading your ad to generate the "I see where you fit into my life response".

As a general rule, all media should be considered against the mindset of the audience. Because if you know what state of mind the audience is in then you can orientate your sales message to breakthrough into that mindset.

As highlighted earlier, few media offer you more than a top-level demographic analysis of their medium – for example, the number of readers, their gender, their age and their location. How this gives any understanding as to the mindset of the audience is a mystery.

And yet the editorial team know exactly what their audience thinks and feels. The trouble is they never talk to the advertising department (they often wish they didn't exist actually) so for you as an advertiser to get any flavour of the psychographic profile of a medium you have to either do it yourself or get your agency to do it.

If understanding the mindset of your audience is key to selling, then understanding the mindset at the time a medium is consumed is of paramount importance and needs to be core to your media planning.

Local Press

So having identified perhaps that, as with national press, you are buying space in someone else's building where you have no control over who comes and goes, and the business-owner doesn't care – why not go local?

There are two types of local newspapers: paid-for and free. Each comes with a different profile. The paid-for papers work much the same as the nationals but obviously are far more community-based. This leads to a much greater separation between the ad sales department and the editorial department so the link to psychographic profiling is much harder. Many of the articles are written by local writers whose focus is local news rather than creating an environment for sales. As a result your ad will be less likely to appear in an area that fits with the Brand Bucket® methodology.

As for the free newspapers – or "free sheets", as they are more commonly termed – these are further still from the decision-making process, and because their distribution is far less controlled it is even harder to match to the psychographic profile of the reader. One thing we do know is that these titles tend to have readers who have less money and more time and are often older as a result. Delivery boys rarely enjoy going up long driveways to post one free newspaper through a letterbox and busy people are less inclined to grab one from a newsstand.

Local newspapers are good for Image Match and Facts Match as when they are read they are considered, and, of course, they come with that all important local flavour.

Radio

The great thing about radio is there is very little you can't do in production terms. In the 80s, Talkback Productions produced a recording to highlight this. It told of how they planned to fill the Grand Canyon with cream and drop a giant cherry on top. After 30 seconds they had done it and listeners had a spoon at the ready.

Well-written scripts can take you almost anywhere, and provide an easy way to give inanimate objects real personality. This medium is great for Awareness and Image Match in that respect. Also, with radio you can choose when to air your commercial, and with a wide spread of radio stations with different listening profiles you can tailor your campaign to have a decent sweet spot amongst your prospects.

The risk is that the listener is hearing your commercial whilst doing something else at home, driving in the car or listening at work. It means that your commercial is only partially heard or absorbed. The broadcast media-owner's dream. Run more ads. The real world will swamp your message in no time.

So you still need a decent budget and a radio campaign in isolation is not as effective without some visual support for your product or service.

Radio is good for announcing events, opening days or special price promotions, and can drive people into test drives well.

Also, this medium is supported by a fantastic industry body, the Radio Advertising Bureau (RAB), who are continuously selling the merits of the medium, bringing real value to their members.

Door Drops

This is the term for all the stuff that comes through your letterbox, whether with your post or in batches, or with your free newspaper.

This medium remains very effective at getting right to your target market (i.e. householders) and is a considered medium (if only between the front door mat and the recycling waste bin). The trouble is, it is a numbers game because there is no way of knowing if your target is in the market for your product or service at the time you drop your leaflet through their door. Some will be and if you send out enough with the right message on them, you might even get a response. Again the Brand Bucket® metric tool will help you identify how many leaflets you need to drop to get a customer and from this you can work out you return on investment.

Essentially, there are three ways to deliver your leaflets:

1. Royal Mail – this is the most expensive and it has the least flexibility (6 weeks lead time), but it is the most effective as it goes with the post that we all at least glance at and it can be named to the householder personally.

2. Door Drop – hand delivery with often no more than three other items, which can be almost done daily. Again, this has to be picked up by the householder, so a simple clear message can be effective.

3. Via local free newspaper – this is the cheapest way to send out leaflets because the newspapers are being delivered anyway. Often the leaflets are inserted in the paper, so if the householder doesn't read the paper the leaflet is never seen. Also, the leaflet is in a very busy environment when placed in a newspaper.

Magazines

The high quality of print in magazines has always held real appeal for the advertiser, and because these are a higher-value purchase than a daily newspaper, they are generally much more considered.

Indeed they will be retained and read in much greater detail and therefore provide a good environment for businesses to advertise their wares. In addition the psychographic profile of the reader is much easier to evaluate because the editors of these titles are much more in tune with their readers.

Also, the look and feel of the magazine is held in much greater esteem than in the newspapers, so editorial and advertising sales work much more closely together. A good magazine will already act as a top of the bucket filter for your business and provide only readers who are more likely to be attracted to your value proposition. As a result it is worth working closely with the magazine team to enable you to move straight to Facts Match or even Response in your advertising.

As the magazines become more specialist or directed towards a specific trade then the magazine is working very hard in your favour and as a result you can go for long copy ads with plenty of benefits because the readers are likely to thank you for the extra information.

Direct Mail

In these days of electronic this and digital that, getting a personally addressed piece of post has a real cachet about it and direct mail has all the potential to do this.

Direct Mail is at its best when it offers a strong Facts Match/ Response approach. The trouble is, too many businesses treat direct mail as a broadcast medium for awareness, and for most of us that means putting it in the file marked "bin".

Consequently direct mail has fallen away somewhat amongst the smaller brands who see it as too expensive. The great thing about DM is that you can measure how many pieces you send out and how many replies you get and from those how many customers you get.

Well-crafted direct mail campaigns can really drive responses and can be targeted reasonably cheaply with good lists from list brokers.

Promotions

This is a marketing approach that invariably demonstrates the least amount of thinking when it comes to demonstrating a value proposition. All too often a promotion is used to raise awareness. Whether a sampling or giveaway or competition or free draw, it always seems as if the promotion itself is more important than persuading people to go and buy the product.

If you are going to run a promotion, then make damn sure that whatever the "creative" approach you use, it at least leaves the participant with a sense of one of your benefits and why they should put buying you ahead of the competitors. Aim for your promotion to act only at Response on The Brand Bucket[®].

Exhibitions

The exhibition industry should be rubbing its hands with anticipation because this is a medium that should be enjoying a new-found place in the marketing arena.

It has all the perfect criteria to get people deep into The Brand Bucket®.

Firstly they are themed, and when well publicised should promise everything people interested in that subject could want to know. That qualification is perfect for the brand-owner. The trouble is, almost no exhibition organiser can actually describe who is attending their next event. They fall foul of the same issue as the broadcast media. Demographics. Because all they want to do is fill a space with exhibitors and then hope people will turn up.

Finding the right exhibition for your product or service should create some of the best leads you can have.

Networking – now this is an important one!

If you are not networked then you are missing out on a significant marketing tool which is driving more business every single day. Why? Well, the trouble with this amazing information age is that nobody has solved some basic limitations.

There are only 24 hours in a day and we all need to sleep some of that time. If you are not a workaholic, then you need some hours to earn a bit of money so you can enjoy the time that is left which is always far less time than you wish. Now this is the time you can spend with other people you like and might even call themselves your friends and family.

To make the most of our free time we need to navigate the information overload that prevents us from getting to our free time. That's on top of the red tape, irrelevant emails, human resource issues, and general "running a business" stuff.

We have already established that the human brain is a

fantastic filter tool as it works continuously to guide us through the day-to-day routine of business as well as having to cross the road as well! So the brain can help us filter out what we don't want, but how good is it at telling us what we *do* want? Actually it's really good here too, but can only respond to the input – and getting the right input, everything you need, now that is the challenge. Especially when it comes to managing the Brand Bucket® process as you draw prospects into your business and turn them into consumers of your offer.

Networking is actually one of the answers. Why? Because a stepping into a room full of experts in their field is like stepping into a giant brain. All you've got to do is find the right cell and talk to that expert and they will have the answer for you.

· Networkers come in two forms – two types of cell, to continue the "brain" analogy: Hunter Cells and Gatherer Cells. To get the best from a network, you must choose which of the two types you will be yourself.

Hunter Cells

A hunter cell is when you go to a network with a specific problem or need to which you wish to find a solution. Whether it's finding a gardener who knows about a rare plant or an Einstein who can help you get an extra hour in the day by explaining how to travel at the speed of light. The focus is on solving a problem for yourself or your business.

Gatherer Cells

On the other hand, becoming a gatherer cell enables you to attend a networking event with the sole intention of being the solution for others in the room. To do this you need to be very well prepared. You need to profile your ideal prospect. It *cannot* be everyone. You need to develop a script that will help you identify whether a person you met 15 seconds ago falls into your chosen target profile. If you don't, you will spend a valuable ten minutes in a conversation that is not with someone who fits your profile. Six of those in a network event and you will leave the event no further forward than when you arrived, with a handful of business cards that were better off as leaves on the tree.

Successful networkers come away with two or three business cards that represent people with whom they are going to talk to again (and from that get one client!).

Therefore, if your plan is to get one client from any network session, your approach should be directed at getting that one client and not to meet everyone in the room.

A networking session is not a broadcast marketing tool, it is about qualifying everyone there to find the one person you are going to do business with.

Time to apply The Brand Bucket® to your networking.

1. Start with awareness building

Assume you know nobody. Often networks are by invitation and you gravitate towards the person who invited you. Unless they have understood their responsibility to get you introduced to all the right people (and they can only do that if you have explained to them if you are hunting or gathering), they will use you as an endorsement of their role in the network, "And here's my friend who 'I' asked to come along today" (subtext look how clever I am at introducing people to this network).

Make sure they know you are there but give them the confidence that their reputation is safe in your hands but that you are going to network without them. If you become an active member of the network, they will of course be able to reflect in the glory of introducing you later.

So you now know nobody. Learn to introduce yourself

naturally. One way that usually works is "Hello, I'm John, John Smith from such and such organisation. We help you achieve this…"

Do not give your card out.

For a start you have just met, so the relationship is only at Step One of The Brand Bucket$^®$, and secondly you'll give away too much information. How you spell your name, your company logo design, your company style, where you are based, if you have a website or twitter address, how you value your business, if you are a start-up, are you a cheapskate or overpriced. All from a business card. Surely not. Most certainly, when someone says "Oh, you're just round the corner from us", "You look like a fashion house", "Oh, you're an accountant" then your conversation is already doomed! Why? Because they have now qualified you and the power in the conversation is with them.

Business cards should only be given out as you part company, but more of that later.

2. Match your image to their image

Don't forget, the key objective is to get the prospect to at least think, if not say, "Ah, I see where you fit into my life." They've already decided if they like you or not by the way you are dressed, what you are drinking and how you introduced yourself and if you are nervous, confident or over confident.

Now business is not about being liked so you have to override any impression you have created by just being yourself and by conveying a promise about your business offer. This should simply be an emotional statement so people can actually say I like what you are saying.

This one thing you say will determine whether the person you are meeting will become a client or not.

No pressure then.

Many people will have come across the idea of a sales pitch, or its shortened form, the "elevator pitch" – where the concept has to be presented in the duration of a lift-ride. (Most elevator pitches not only make the buttons in an elevator more interesting, they make you want to get out of elevator on the second floor even if you are going to the 10th.) There are many variants of this: "60-second" networking; positioning statements; mission statements; the brand consultant's turn of phrase.

The trouble with most of those approaches is that they all portray the service or product from a company-out perspective. Now that can be interesting, but the listener still has to work out what's in it for them.

So after introducing who you are and who you represent, the next thing you say should be something your listener will respond to with a "Now that's something I/we need." If they don't react that way, exit from the conversation and start again with someone else. Don't worry about offending them. They should be there to network too, so wasting time with you is not what they want anyway. The only rules to this are if they have done likewise and said something that makes *you* say "Ah, that's something I need," you need to flip from hunter to gatherer. Don't forget to go back though.

Creating this introductory statement is not easy but here are a few approaches you might consider:

1. How you are revolutionising a service, market or product.
2. Your personal vision for what you are doing.
3. A killer fact about a gap in the market that inspires you.

Most networking events provide badges. This is seen as a hygiene factor for running a networking event. Sometimes they are pre-printed but only if you've pre-registered. Human error can often get the spelling of your name wrong – miss out the company name and this certainly won't help communicate your proposition! Empty badge-holders are cheap to buy and with a little work on the computer you can soon have a decent looking badge which has your name, company logo and, if you are really brave, a short message about your business. If you wear this, not only will you stand out but you'll demonstrate forethought to your prospect and give them extra information to help you qualify them.

3. Get those Facts Match benefits out

You are "suited and booted" or "a hardy in a cardi" and you are introduced to a new contact. You have ventured into the most important part of networking, creating a valued relationship for your prospect.

Now is *not* the time to go on a fishing trip by listing out all the **features** of your business in the hope that someone says "Oh I'm looking for an accountant, lawyer, marketing expert."

This is the time you must portray your business in terms of **benefits**, something that the prospect might find useful. This is not an elevator pitch either, this is a simple here's something that might interest you that we offer.

Whatever you say at this point the aim is to get people to say "That's something I'm looking for." If they don't say that, then move on to the next prospect. If they do, qualify them by finding out why they think they need you. Your sole focus at this time is to get to the next step.

4. Gain a commitment by getting them to respond

The only person who can pitch at a networking meeting is the person running the networking event itself (if they want people to come back).

The sole aim of networking is to get people into a one-to-one situation where you are in full control of the meeting. The tone of this meeting should appear non-committal for the prospect. It is also where you are going to place the most significant investment in the acquisition process, so you need to be sure that whatever you are giving away has a better than 50% chance of leading to a paying customer.

In this one-to-one session you will bring to life your benefits and demonstrate how using your product or service will help them get more out of their business (or even their life).

I promise this session will be invigorating because it is the moment when you know a sale will happen and there is a real buzz when someone else buys what you produce.

So sell the benefits in this "test drive" of your offer and go for closure. Get the prospect to acknowledge that they would like to participate in your one-to-one session. If they do, your job is done. Time to exit. Offer your card and ask for their contact details in return.

Most people will either forget or run out of business cards at networking events so take some blanks that they can fill out for you and take spare pens too, ones that are nice to write with ideally.

By this time you should have obtained contact details and left the prospect with some expectation of what will happen next. They should be in no doubt what you will do with their information. Explain that you will contact them either by phone or email within 24/48 hours to find a satisfactory time to meet again. Advise who they will be hearing from and who they will be meeting and how long it will take.

Remember give, give, give without conditions.

5. Follow up, it's key to Usage

So now you've done the easy bit, this is where the real work starts. Most networkers think their "networking" has finished now they have made a definitive connection with a prospect.

You cannot be more wrong.

Some networkers leave an event with three or four business cards; good networkers leave with scribbled notes, cards, people they are going to link to other people, emails they promised to write.

The trouble is that when they empty their jacket pockets the following day a random mêlée of possibilities falls onto their desk. To satisfy themselves they will pick one or at best two to do something about there and then. And with an email winding its way through that other network, the internet, they get on with their day job.

Now if you are that lucky one who was chosen to be contacted straight away then you can ignore the next bit but let's assume you are not. Your card is sitting in a little pile called "I'll do those later". This pile looks remarkably like last week's "I'll do that later" pile and the one from the event before. You get the picture. The thing about network connections is that they decay within hours, so you can guarantee that all the energy you put into giving away your contact details will become part of background noise within 48 hours tops.

So here's a rule: if you actively network, allocate one hour in your diary the following morning for follow-up. This hour is probably the most valuable hour you will spend in your networking life. Make yourself a hot drink. Clear your desk and empty your jacket pockets onto the table.

Imagine you are staring at 10% of your annual turnover. Actually this is possibly the most exciting part of networking. You now have gained permission to talk to all the people on your desk. It is the ultimate "opt-in". All of the cards are screaming talk to me, sell to me, make me richer and I'll make you richer. It's a marketing wow. Pick each contact up and stare at it. In your hand is a key to a whole new network, one you know nothing about.

Ivan Misner, who founded BNI, hypothesises that every person connects with at least 200 businesses. If you have 10 cards that means 2000 possible connections. Stare at the card hard, it's probably worth millions of pounds of business. Not to you directly but that's one hell of an investment fund to see if a little of it could come your way. Add the card details to a database. A simple Word or Excel spreadsheet is all you need. If you are a bit cleverer use Access, Act or Salesforce or check out online for collaborative platforms such as www.basecamphq.com.

Capture everything, how you remember that person you met, what they said they were interested in and what you promised them. Do this for all the cards. Do not make calls, write emails or react to any of them. **You must capture the data first.** When it is finished you have just created a key asset in your business and freed up your mind.

You can now throw away all those cards! Here's a suggestion though: get a large bucket and throw them in there as if you were entering a competition at an exhibition. Then once a week dip your hand in and pull one out and drop them a line to see how they are, or send them a tip or invite them to dinner. Be amazed at the response.

Now every connection has a lifespan. Some are short, opportunistic connections. You have an immediate need and this connection will potentially meet that need. They should be followed up quickly with a clarification of the benefit of talking further and very soon. Aim for a one-to-one meeting soon. A short great-to-meet-you, I'd-like-to-specifically-discuss-"such-and-such"-with-you.

Other connections are for building new routes to market. They require a better understanding of each other's businesses and this will require some investment of time.

An email to these people should be considered and provide the recipient a better understanding of how your business can benefit their business and how you see this working reciprocally. Let your value proposition shine through. Aim for an extended "chemistry meeting", a no-obligation meeting to establish corporate philosophy. If both of you are going to put your reputations on the line you need to be sure that the value propositions of both work in harmony. These are the most important connections. They will grow your business and make it stronger.

Name	Where Met	Business Type	Test Drive Meeting (Call)	One to one Meeting (email)	Stay in touch
John Smith	Chamber	Accountant			✓
Joe Bloggs	Chamber	Lawyer		✓	
A.N.Other	Network X	Marketing Agent	✓		

Finally there are the connections that are the "honeypot" connections. These connections are the most exciting – so much so that they jump off the desk at you, pirouette mid-air, and wink at you knowingly.

Someone has built a business that **you** know will change the way you do business and if you link to their business you'll be a multimillionaire inside 18 months. They'll know this from the way you talked excitedly about working together. But they are the honeypot and you are the bee. You'll need to be thick-skinned because that old honeypot is surrounded by other bees that sting. Now you can live with one or two stings but over time this relationship is going to hurt too much and if you've taken your eye off your own business it might just kill you! These people need to be invited to a one-to-one meeting.

A bee's sting kills the bee so they sting only as a last resort, when they feel really threatened. If you are to follow a 'honeypot' strategy be aware that other businesses will often take you down with them if they see you buzzing into their honeypot.

Make sure with all this valuable data you have collected, that you follow up every lead, qualify it again, arrange the meetings and make the onward connections.

6. Stay in touch and build loyalty

Many leads will peter out and not really lead to immediate entropy for your business. But you have established a relationship with these people, you've qualified them (twice) and although you cannot do business with them straight away you need to keep the relationship alive. Why? Because you now exist in their world and if you've handled it right you will have become part of their image dimensions – how they see themselves.

Stay in touch with these people. If you do they will add your reputation to their own and that can generate new business at any time!

Social Networking

This is a new phenomenon in real terms and for marketeers is a totally unproven medium. Undoubtedly there will be successes but equally there are more likely to be failures. This is true of all new emerging media. That said, this approach to marketing must come with a serious health warning because the power of the medium is amongst those who use it rather than the media-owner. The resulting fluidity puts the control of your message at real risk of being entirely discredited in one click of the "submit" button based on one individual's perception of your business. Equally of course your business can become an instantaneous success in one click too, but few businesses are geared to cope with this and fail soon after a false peak in sales.

The other key weakness in the current social networking infrastructure is that the context of communication is misleading. If communication is 20% verbal and 80% non-verbal and modus operandi is essentially written, then much of what we draw on to convey or receive a message is totally absent from this medium. As a result, without the context of the Brand Bucket® steps, any views expressed through social networks online will be out of context and therefore from a marketing perspective unreliable. A few bad experiences and we will all simply use social networking for exactly what the term suggests – social networking between friends, i.e. people you know. Now wait a minute... do I really need to go online to communicate with them about brands?

Cold Calls

The blight of anybody who hates answering the phone, cold calling is an important part of the brand relationship – and handled well, it can pay dividends.

The art of outbound calling is to remember that you are

working at the Image Match level not the Response level. Using calls to quantify how people are feeling about the area in which your product or service operates will create openings to invite people into a test drive through certain benefits.

A cold caller should be a brand expert with full understanding of your Brand Bucket® journey. No scripts just a good understanding of the key messages at each level, and let it be natural. Hopefully it will cut out the "how are you today" or "we're updating our out-of-date database", both guaranteed to elicit abuse. Try "we understand you might be interested in..."

Search Engines

Over 40% of us regularly use search engines and when we do over 90% use either Google or Yahoo, so search engines are really important for today's marketers.

That said, you need a decent website that is not full of "tell" messaging but is a gigantic invite to make contact.

There are two types of search engine listing: the free organic listing and the pay-per-click listing. Every day the number of websites in the world doubles so staying at the top of the first page organically is a full-time effort that requires a scientific approach to using keywords, metatags, alt tags, web links, no flash, no dropdown menus, dynamic text, video content, where your server is located, compliance, the list goes on and on. The trouble with organic listings is that once again you have no real control of your marketing using this method, and unless you are very niche the chances are your ranking will move around the listing all the time.

The alternative is to pay to be on the front page. Pay-per-click is currently one of the most powerful marketing tools in market today. Again successful use of this medium is a science too, otherwise you'll soon see your bank balance diminishing without real return. This is because the medium is marketed demographically, the more clicks the more likely you are to yield customers. Don't forget Adam Smith. Google are only in it for them, not you!

Pay-per-click works at its best when used psychographically as outlined earlier in chapter 5. **Create a click on me only if you match our psychographic profile.** Already the prospects coming through the top of your bucket are qualified!

Point of Sale

Point of Sale does not mean the point at which the sale takes place. This is usually called the till or checkout. No, this is the final opportunity to influence the purchase decision and is so often wasted by brand-owners. A list of features at this point is really the last thing a buyer wants. With so much choice directly in front of them, they are already confused. What the hell, let's confuse them some more! More of this and less of that and a bit of the other. In the end the prospect will buy the cheapest or the most attractive, hardly the stuff of long-term relationships. So close and yet so far. This is not the time for your bucket to spring a leak. Try demonstrating benefits one last time and be amazed by the effect on your sales.

Packaging

Often the first real point of engagement post purchase, packaging should be a full endorsement of why you are such great value.

A sheet of tissue in your folded shirt, a heavy set box for one silver charm from the Pandora range, the iphone box with its integrated sim-card key, a high value carrier from a fashion retailer swung with pride as the purchaser leaves the shop. All examples of packaging that makes you feel great about your purchase. **Make your packaging part of your marketing and see the effect.**

User Guides

Go on, walk the extra mile and treat your user guide as a piece of added value. Car manufacturers have worked this out but have the white goods manufacturers, the brown goods manufacturers or the banks, insurance companies or providers of IT equipment? Other than the product itself, user guides are often ignored. And yet they are second only to the product itself in frequency of use.

****

Of course there are literally thousands of touchpoints for your business but the shortlist outlined above is there just to get you to think about each one you use to engage with your prospects and customers. With Brand Bucket® thinking to hand you can easily turn each and every point of engagement to your advantage and build real differentiation into your brand relationship.

12

POSTSCRIPT

The Brand Bucket® approach outlined in this book, if adopted in its entirety, will bring genuine rewards to your business by making your marketing work.

In continual use every day it directs many businesses towards a stronger brand relationship with their prospects, ensuring future prosperity from them as long-term consumers.

The changed state that the discipline of marketing now finds itself in has proven to be the making of The Brand Bucket® methodology which is seeing greater impact on businesses of all shapes and sizes.

By starting with your value proposition you have the foundation of a relationship. When combined with a psychographic profile of your ideal prospect you have a meeting of mindset that, handled in an orderly manner, will yield a long-term relationship which by its very nature and constituent elements will be differentiated and unique.

It is the discipline of marketing that will bind the business story to the consumer and enable sales.

With your value proposition to hand you can audit all of the engagement points with your business from the shop floor to the board room. By aligning all of these touchpoints to the key value drivers from your value proposition you will minimise marketing waste and boost the bottom line through more profitable sales.

The Brand Bucket® is your guide, it is a way of thinking, a

methodology that will work time and time again, providing links, checks and measurable activities that add real power to your marketing.

Each step a prospect takes through Awareness, Image Match, Facts Match, Response, Usage and Loyalty will bring value into your business in the form of future sales, ongoing sales and repeat sales.

You'll preserve more of your cash if your marketing is sales-directed because the focus on the numbers will give you access to your cost per acquisition (CPA) and very quickly you'll see the value in the results that your marketing efforts deserve.

This book has challenged a number of conventions. If it has stirred you to adapt some of your thinking or change the way you approach things then welcome.

If it hasn't, then thank you for getting this far and do pass it on to someone who you feel might benefit from this proven approach.

May your Brand Bucket® fill as you make your marketing work.

Barnaby Wynter

Visit: www.thebrandbucket.com and register for free for news, views and to do's related to this book.

APPENDIX
HOW MARKETING HAS CHANGED:
A BRIEF HISTORY

In 1439 Johannes Gutenberg invented the first printing press and by 1593 Caxton was producing the first newssheets. To pay for this, Caxton would ask local tradesmen – butchers, bakers and candlestick-makers – to take some space in his newssheet. He would set their name and what they sold and more people would come to buy things from them. Very quickly all the butchers, bakers and candlestick-makers wanted to be in these newspapers and a network of sales agents had to go and collect the money and get basic details. These "Advertising Agents" were paid by commission set at the time at 15%. It soon became very popular as everyone wanted to be involved in these new ways of communication.

A new dynamic came into play. By this time, all the expertise in setting up the printing machines was with the printers, so it was they who would create the advertisements, and most were broadly the same with only a name change. Advertisers soon realised they were spending money to simply say the same thing as their competitors so they started asking their advertising agents if they could have something different from the others. It was the first time "creativity" emerged as a tool for making ads work. The printers were not interested in having ideas that differentiated the ads so the advertising agents became advertising agencies where ideas were developed to make each ad a little different from each other.

And so it was for hundreds of years with more and more newspapers appearing across the globe. The advertising industry grew exponentially and all was very calm. Then a man called John Logie Baird invented something that was going to change world order. On 2nd October 1925 he broadcast the first moving pictures (from Frith Street in Central London) and the television was born.

Here was a new medium that got to a broader audience and soon advertisers were able to put their messages between the programmes.

The first TV commercial broadcast in the UK was at 8:12pm on September 22nd 1955 during a variety show and was for Gibbs SR toothpaste. It was only the first commercial by chance as there had been a 23-company lottery including Guinness, Surf, National Benecol, Brown & Polson Custard and Summer Country Magazine.

The use of sound and moving images was of course to revolutionise advertising. Once again the skills to populate a short time frame were with a select few. The film-makers. They soon realised they could supplement their income and pay for what they really wanted to do (make full-length films) by making the commercials. Fortunately for the advertising agencies, they were not interested in understanding what makes people want to buy a box of detergent, a bag of frozen peas or a new car. So the advertising agencies grew from strength to strength.

It was the time of the consumer. As business-owners invented and created new ways to make and sell goods they could ramp up manufacture and put their new idea on television. Literally millions of people would see this announcement and go and find the advertised product in the shops.

Putting your product on television meant you could reach millions of people all at the same time. It was a numbers game as people would sit and watch wall-to-wall TV from teatime to bedtime. Big numbers; big budgets; big sales. It helped boost other broadcast media too: radio, press and cinema and even posters enjoyed new-found status as the advertising industry led by Madison Avenue in New York and agencies in London attracted some of the advertising greats many of whom we still talk of today.

The world of "above the line" advertising was born.

"Above the line" was originally an accounting term applied by the broadcast media who worked to a formula of 15% commission. Thus the media-owner received 85% and the agency 15% of the agreed advertising price. So for a £100,000 campaign the agency would receive £15,000. Very quickly advertising agencies became solely focused on broadcast media. It was a great way of making money. So any medium that could be charged out with a commission was classed as "above the line". All other forms of advertising – print, direct marketing, exhibitions, point of sale – were classed as "below the line" because they were quoted with a margin in the price. Often this margin was much larger than 15% because the quantities were much lower, and the human effort involved in getting the materials to the prospect much greater.

In the UK, the marketing communications industry grew rapidly with the creation of above-the-line advertising agencies that made lots of money with TV commercials and press ads and below-the-line agencies that made far less money. They were often derided by those in the fancy suits and driving the fancy cars and eating in the fancy restaurants. Theirs was a position assured. They commanded big fees for creating mini films, images and copy that yielded big sales.

Bill Bernbach once famously wrote *"Don't tell my mother I work in advertising, tell her I'm playing the piano in a whorehouse."* A clever inversion of the criticism that was often levelled at the admen who were clearly cashing in for what seemed, from the outside, an easy job.

The early days were simple. As businesses took their products onto television an adoring public would serve up the frozen pea, go to work on an egg, get there well with shell, smile with toothpaste confidence, drink the Guinness stout that might be good for you, wash whiter than white, and drive reliable, safe, fast cars.

And so the Unique Selling Point (USP) was born. As more and more competitive products were given a voice each one took a unique aspect of their offer and created a differentiated position around it.

Today the concept of the USP is almost totally dead but more of that later.

Buy the end of the 60s the advertising industry really dominated the marketing mix, hoovering up the biggest share of the marketing budget. As more and more businesses used advertising, a new dimension entered the industry. Distinguishing between the different agencies was becoming harder. After all anyone can have an idea so who was to say one agency was any better that another? A new breed of agency emerged or more specifically a new discipline in the agency was born – planning, purportedly to add a little science to the gut feel that admen had traditionally traded on by undertaking research amongst customers about what they thought.

At around this time, the USP evolved into the "single-minded proposition" (originally attributed to Stanley Pollitt, founder of the agency Boase Massimi Pollitt in 1968). As products and services became harder to distinguish from each other, the planners used research amongst users and non-users to find out new reasons to buy.

These reasons were distilled down into a single statement that the "Planner" believed would be sufficiently motivating to make people buy that product or service. This was the beginning of the end for the USP, as it meant that even more businesses could advertise their wares, even though they had something very similar to a competitor.

Combined with this, technology and mass manufacturing led us from **the consumer age** where there was really only limited choice into the **post consumerist age** we see today where there is an eye-watering array of alternative choices.

No longer could you just buy the big box of Persil that your mother always used; now there were many variants of Persil, liquids, micro powder, tablets as well as the same variants from the competitors too all with their own message.

As a result the ad agencies were given new life. Now that the creative people were told what they had to say rather than told what product they had to advertise, they could focus on bringing this message to life in a way that would add a new dynamic to the message. And so creativity moved to a new level. No more voiced-over pictures of woman in kitchen as man gets home from work, but something altogether different.

Before long we had TV commercials that were more interesting than the programmes, press ads that were more thought-provoking than the editorial around them and a real sense that these weren't just infomercials or well written press articles but the start of something else – a new level of relationship between products and services and their clients. It was an era where we saw the emergence of what we now take for granted as "brand".

If advertising was cool before, now it was a dream factory.

Anyone who was creatively minded was attracted to this increasingly exciting industry. The gap between above-the-line advertising and below-the-line marketing grew larger with the creative talent heading above and technicians and specialists moving below the line.

The 70s and 80s saw the creative side of the business become king, giving rise to the likes of David Ogilvy, David Abbott, David Trott and Bill Bernbach amongst many others. (So David became Goliath and it came with a big Bill!).

As advertising spending grew and grew, the media-owners became more powerful too, and before long there were big deals taking place between the media moguls and big agency bosses.

Clients saw their marketing budgets escalate year on year as everyone stuck their nose into the broadcast advertising trough.

By the mid to late 80s in the UK there were 300 big agencies negotiating with 14 different regional TV buying points for literally thousands of products and services all going after a time-limited resource on two TV channels (now 12 minutes allowed in any given hour in the UK).

Populated by big budget films in 10, 20, 30 and 60 second slots, it was the time of the barrow boy in media departments; the intellects in planning; the Oxbridge "smoothies" in client service; the art school graduates in creative; and the technicians in print and production.

But it was a formula for decline.

As each department grew in power they started to believe they really were the cats who had got the cream. With this power came an arrogance that was to see a change in the fortunes in advertising, the results of which we see today.

The first nail in the agency model's coffin was when the barrow boys started to push their weight around and combine the media budgets of different brand-owners to improve their negotiation position for better rates with the media-owners, using this new found media buying power. The "mine is bigger than yours" strategy worked in the early 90s but saw an immediate reaction from the media-owners who combined forces too.

Media Departments merged and set up media independents thereby removing themselves from the creative side of the brand relationship and media-owners combined sales houses until eventually they both simply traded commodities. We saw the rise of newspaper moguls and the emergence of segmented thinking. As the planners refined their target market profiles so they could keep their single-minded proposition thinking intact, they were matched by the media-owners, releasing highly profiled magazines and at the first opportunity creating special interest TV channels.

Still with mass-market thinking, we saw a wave of women's magazines, then men's magazines, then special interest magazines. We saw movie channels, sports channels and news channels leading to a whole range of special interest channels. All were commodity media designed to keep media spends up by providing more quality segmentation and more choice.

The Client sat by and watched. Bewildered by the insights into their customers' behaviours, frightened by the thought that their competitors were doing better than them, and vexed by the escalating costs of advertising.

In 1991, Guinness ran a conference for the benefit of advertising agencies in the Centre Point Tower in London. The speaking "death slot" at 2.15 pm was given by the Finance Director of Guinness. Of the 300 admen and women who were in attendance in the morning, less than 100 made it back from the lunch, being served some 10ft from the lecture theatre.

The message of the next hour was clear.

Advertising budgets were seen as part of marketing spend which appeared under "other miscellaneous items" on the balance sheet. Having endured a recent recession in the late 80s he outlined his role as he received requests from the board to save money to maintain profits and keep shareholders happy.

Looking at the balance sheet and after consideration of costs associated with raw materials, brewing, bottling, distribution and staff, changing the large number appearing next to miscellaneous seemed to have, in theory, the least effect on the ability for Guinness to maintain sales in the short term.

The result: a call to the advertising agency to say their budget had been cut. Now if your business model is an "eat what you bill" commission-based model then this unexpected call is a real blow. At the time this was a call that Guinness rarely made as they truly valued their brand advertising at the time. However this was not so true for most other business-owners however big or small. And yet there is a considerable weight of industry evidence that if you do not maintain a relationship with prospects and customers through the good and the bad times, then your business will simply wither on the vine.

As ad agencies weathered the storm of another recession in the mid 90s they often shed the more expensive craftsmen first, believing that fresh thinking and new ideas from their young (and therefore cheaper) creative departments were what clients needed and wanted. The client was however becoming wary.

The decline in advertising as a lead marketing tool was accelerated further by the people who understood the importance of building a relationship rather than simply creating a piece of cut through advertising. As they lost their jobs in the agencies that were unable to adapt to the changing marketing arena fast enough, they became consultants either working directly with clients or founding niche businesses of their own.

Soon they were undercutting the bigger agencies with more cost-effective ways of marketing, providing better links between spend and results and beginning the process of raising the profile of other marketing tools as effective alternatives to advertising.

This was further accelerated as print technology moved forward. In 1986 Fleet Street, the home of the national newspaper came to a standstill when a man called Rupert Murdoch of News Corporation automated his newspaper printing, moving production to Wapping in East London – following the earlier move there of the *Today* Newspaper run by a man called Eddie Shah who had pioneered and introduced colour into his daily newspaper.

A newspaper with colour. Imagine one without now.

As print technology developed we saw the rise of the brand message on almost everything.

Media madness. (The next wave, digitalisation of print media. The one after that, 2D to 3D. Holograms? You can see it coming.)

The industry in the UK changed beyond all recognition and by the end of the 1990s, 80% of all advertising spend was through the top 5% of UK agencies. The barrow boy mentality caused agencies to merge, often going global, and forcing clients to go for lowest-common-denominator advertising work.

The middle-tier agencies in the UK all but disappeared by merger and acquisition. There is now no middle order to the UK advertising industry. In its place are literally thousands of niche players in the marketing arena.

During the course of this change we have seen the dilution of planning as a force in advertising. Planning-led agencies found that clients were doing much of the work of planners themselves and could brief the agency without the need for a planner. The drive for innovation in cluttered marketplaces meant that clients had to split peas to get that all-important unique selling proposition. The need for expensive, cut-through creative has also declined as the "shout at large groups of people in the hope that some find your product or service desirable" is both nonsensical and wasteful in today's marketing world.

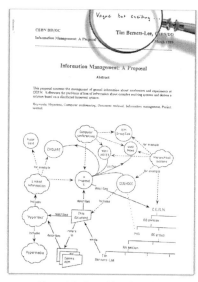

The original world wide web proposal document

The reason for this: **the internet.**

In 1989/90 Mr Tim Berners-Lee created the World Wide Web by suggesting a link-up between hypertext mark up language (HTML) with transmission protocols and the idea of having a domain name.

Very quickly images started appearing on the internet which until then had been a text-only tool used primarily by universities and other public bodies to communicate with each other. The medium took on a new direction. The unregulated access to images inspired the porn industry to develop software and code that underpins much of how we all use the internet today.

This is not something to get stressed about. If prostitution is allegedly one of the oldest "selling" professions in the world, then it is no surprise that human endeavour can be inspired by procreation activities and the web need not be any different.

In many ways it is what has made Yahoo, Google and all the

evolving social networks all that much better as they constantly battle to create better ways to keep unsavoury articles and websites away from innocent eyes.

The combination of the accessibility to computers thanks to International Business Machines (IBM) and the release of their operating systems to enable the likes of Microsoft, enabled the development new ways of building committed relationships between human beings on a scale larger than anyone had previously ever thought possible. (This is not true of Apple Macintosh whose parallel decision to keep their OS system locked has limited human endeavour to less than 10% of computers worldwide and yet, as their ipod, iphone, and ipad technology prove, could have helped revolutionise so many more of our lives!)

By the mid 90s people were piling money into new concepts on the web that appeared to have at their disposal a broadcast medium unmatched by any other.

It was the era for those forgotten technicians in industry to step up to the keyboard. They arose from behind the scenes putting together websites that would revolutionise the way we all led our lives.

There were two problems.

Firstly no-one knew these amazing websites were there and secondly everyone was ignoring the rules of business so carefully nurtured since the industrial revolution.

The ad agencies saw another opportunity to spend more client money blasting broadcasts about this new website and that new website. Technicians are technicians for a reason, and are rarely able to lift their souls from the world of digital code. The "dotcom" bubble grew, funded by the ignorance of venture capital until it burst at the turn of the new century.

The so-called millennium bug never manifested itself as aeroplanes falling from the sky or computers defaulting our bank accounts to 1900 or the shutting down of hospital theatres and defence satellites ceasing to function.

It appeared as the way to make fortunes disappear.

Stock markets declined and new market entrants disappeared as quickly as they arrived. Once again advertising agencies were put under the spotlight, this time not only by clients but also by the investors in those clients.

They were not to recover this time.

This was no simple recession; this was a fundamental shift in the understanding of how advertising really influenced people's propensity to buy. The big agencies focused on global activity and left their UK clients behind. The big clients like Unilever sold off their "local market" brands and unified their marketing efforts on a global basis abandoning traditional advertising almost entirely.

The larger medium-sized agencies, with predominantly UK-based client bases, were simply swallowed up by the big fish or disappeared entirely. *Campaign*, the industry trade magazine, dropped their Top 300 annual agency list and now only publishes the Top 100 as the agency world became so fragmented.

Clients themselves were taking back their marketing budgets or demanding more and more from their ad agency. The ad agencies had little more to give.

The whole approach of single-minded propositions pushed out through broadcast media was no longer effective because no single medium could guarantee the coverage needed to make this work.

With more TV channels, more magazines, more websites, and just as importantly print technology to enable your message to appear on almost anything, suddenly the need to understand how people gather their information to help them make buying decisions became key. Few in the advertising agency world had the training to meet this demand.

Another step-change in the way consumers gather their information was the search engine. Gathering more and more pace in the late 90s the search engine has come into its own in the new century. With access to a computer for those who want it more or less universal, most people use a search engine result to guide them in their decision-making.

Type in a keyword and a new world of information opens up before you. Everything you could possibly ever need! All too often much of what you need is hidden behind out of date, irrelevant information you don't need.

Because the search engine is a technician's paradise we were once again immersed in code-led information overload.

Typing in "bank rate" gets over 170 million results in 0.31 seconds. Typing in "potato" gets 35 million results in 0.18 seconds. Typing in "air" gets 783 million results in 0.21 seconds. The clever technicians at Google saw the power in this information and whilst they created "natural organic ranked listings" to make their system appealing, it has become too clumsy.

Because these rankings place reliance on the number of times a relevant word appears in your site, it is still possible that a website posted in 1998 will be ranked top. To address this Google created a paid-for medium where they present your listing at the top based on what you will pay them every time someone types in a keyword and then clicks on a link you've written. These "sponsored links" are how Google makes its money. Yahoo does much the same.

This has changed how businesses can market themselves and more importantly how consumers behave when seeking out new products and services. No longer do consumers wait to be told of new offers; they effectively ask for someone to sell to them.

And the ad agency answer to this? Carry on blasting the prospect with a big-budget loud hailer and a single-minded proposition. Draw your own conclusion as to whether this will work.

So where to next?

The last five years have seen a new phenomenon in marketing. With the broadcast industry on its knees, with anything that can be printed on carrying a message, with information overload from the web, we are seeing a return to the forefront of one of the most powerful tools ever created: word of mouth.

In May 2009 247 billion emails were being sent every day (Radicati Group)

As the mobile phone usage changed into texting and we saw the use of email explode, communication using keyboards became far more acceptable.[4] In the new century this is being formalised in the form of online networking tools.

In this book there is a section on how to get the most from networks, but from a history point of view we now see networking going on everywhere.

Businesses are driving this, evolving online through the likes of Facebook[5], Linked-in, Twitter, eBay, Betfair, Skype, among many others. These tools are changing the way we communicate with each other as they are defined by users.

---

[4] The first email was sent between 2 computers next to each other in 1971 by Ray Tomlinson and was entitled QWERTYUIOP. The first mass email was sent out by the Advanced Research Projects Agency Networks (ARPANET) a US Military organisation to 600 users. It was badly received and thwarted any future mass emails for some years after. The first SPAM!

[5] On 21st July 2010 Facebook claimed to have topped 500 Million users making it the largest online social network globally according to the New York Times. In the same article a recent survey by the American Customer Satisfaction Index showed that user satisfaction with Facebook stood at 64 on a 100-point scale, which placed it in the bottom 5 percent of the companies covered in the index.

As these communication platforms take on more people, they morph into something else.

Although they enable global conversations, they lack the responsibility and control that face-to-face word of mouth brings and so a new phase in marketing has begun: **face-to-face network marketing.**

There are a whole spectrum of these sites from BNI, BRE, Chamber of Commerce, Netlinked, 4Networking, Athena, Women in Business up to the likes of Vistage and other exclusive member only groups.

Marketing that used to take place in the pub is now formalised into fit-for-purpose networking tools where people can access peer-to-peer knowledge to guide them through the decision-making process required to make an informed purchase.

When communication between human beings is 20% verbal and 80% non verbal we must question the long-term effectiveness of the written word through online network tools.

If consumers are now willing to request information and ask for help rather than rely on being told what's right for them, then marketing must be undertaken differently.

The broadcast rules no longer apply.

The appeal of your value must now be portrayed in an entirely different way. It must be marketed correctly.

The history tells us this.

The Brand Bucket® methodology tells us too.

INDEX

ABOUT THE AUTHOR

After receiving a BSc Honours degree in Psychology in 1985, Barnaby Wynter took simultaneous Postgraduate Diplomas, one in Advertising and one in Marketing. He followed this with a three-month work experience scheme at the top 40 advertising agency, Lonsdale's.

From there he joined a small agency Reid Walker Advertising to help launch the Fiat Fiorino and Fiat Ducato. This gave him enough experience to join the team at Ogilvy and Mather Advertising (O&M) to work on the TV launch of the Ford Sierra and Ford Granada, later being promoted to the launches of Radion, Argos, Birds Eye Healthy Options, Birds Eye Steakhouse and Liptonice. It was at O&M where his love affair with the internet began after downloading one of the first pictures on the internet. (It took 53 minutes and was of a kettle on a lab bench).

After almost six years, Barnaby left O&M to improve his understanding of the creative process and worked for three years each at two other agencies Reay Keating Hamer (becoming Mellors Reay) and Walsh Trott Chick Smith, launching brands such as Boots Opticians, Red Stripe Lager, Woodpecker Red, Toshiba Home Cinema, *Sunday Express* and First Telecom.

In 1999 Barnaby joined his current company as MD combining his knowledge of the internet and big brand experience to manage the launch of E*Trade in the UK and Europe. The last ten years have included rebranding, launches and the ongoing marketing for the likes of Marie Curie Cancer Care, The Children's

Society, Bookham Technology, Deutsche Post, Classic FM, The Royal College of Obstetricians and Gynaecologists among 250 brands, start-ups and NASDAQ and FTSE businesses.

Barnaby is regularly published in trade magazines and online business websites.